how2become

A London Underground Train Driver

The Insider's Guide

Orders: Please contact How2become Ltd, Suite 2, 50 Churchill Square Business Centre, Kings Hill, Kent ME19 4YU.

Telephone: (44) 0845 643 1299 - Lines are open Monday to Friday 9am until 5pm. Fax: (44) 01732 525965. You can also order via the e mail address info@how2become.co.uk.

ISBN: 9781910602249

First published 2015

Typeset for How2become Ltd by Good Golly Design, Canada, goodgolly.ca

Printed in Great Britain for How2become Ltd by: CMP (uk) Limited, Poole, Dorset.

CONTENTS

INTRODUCTION

Dear Sir/Madam,

Welcome to *How2Become a London Underground Train Driver*: The Insider's Guide. This guide has been designed to help you prepare for and pass the London Underground Train Driver selection process. We feel certain that you will find the guide both a comprehensive and highly informative tool for helping you obtain one of the most sought after careers available.

The London Underground selection process is drawn out and highly competitive. On average, there are 300 to 400 applicants for every vacancy. Coupled with the fact that posts are rarely advertised, this makes it an even harder job to obtain. However, do not let this put you off. Many of the applicants who do apply are grossly under prepared, and they normally fail at the first hurdle. You must prepare fully if you are to pass the selection process and be offered a position as a London Underground Train Driver. There are a number of things that you can do in order to increase your chances of success, and they are all contained within this guide.

If you would like any further assistance with the selection process then we offer the following products and training courses via the website www.how2become.com:

Finally, you won't achieve much in life without hard work, determination and perseverance. Work hard, stay focused and be what you want!

Good luck and best wishes,

The how2become team

The How2become team

PREFACE
By Author Richard McMunn

Before I get into the guide and teach you how to prepare for the London Underground Train Driver selection process, it is important that I explain a little bit about my background and why I am qualified to help you succeed.

I joined the Royal Navy soon after leaving school and spent four fabulous years in the Fleet Air Arm branch onboard HMS Invincible. It had always been my dream to become a Firefighter, and I only ever intended on staying at the Royal Navy for the minimum amount of time. At the age of 21 I left the Royal Navy and joined Kent Fire and Rescue Service. Over the next 17 years I had an amazing career with a fantastic organisation. During that time I was heavily involved in training and recruitment, often sitting on interview panels and marking application forms for those people who wanted to become Firefighters. I also worked very hard and rose to the rank of Station Manager. I passed numerous assessment centres during my time in the job and I estimate that I was successful at over 95% of interviews I attended.

The reason for my success was not because I am special in anyway, or that I have lots of educational qualifications, because I don't! In the build up to every job application or promotion I always prepared myself thoroughly. I found a formula that worked and that is what I intend to teach you throughout the duration of this book.

Over the past few years I have taught many people how to pass the selection process for becoming a London

Underground Train Driver, both through this guide and also during my one day intensive training courses. Each and every one of the students who attends my course is determined to pass, and that is what you will need to do too if you are to be successful. As you are probably aware many people want to become London Underground Train Drivers. As a result of this, the competition is fierce. However, the vast majority of people who do apply will submit poor application forms or they will do very little to prepare for the assessment centre and the interviews. As a result, they will fail.

The way to pass the selection process is to embark on a comprehensive period of intense preparation. I would urge you to use an action plan during your preparation. This will allow you to focus your mind on exactly what you need to do in order to pass. For example, if it has been many years since you last attended an interview, then you will probably have a lot of work to do in this area. If it has been many years since you last sat a test, then you may have to work very hard in order to pass the psychometric tests that form part of the assessment centre. The point I am making here, is that it is within your power to improve on your weak areas. If you use an action plan then you are far more likely to achieve your goals.

I use action plans in just about every element of my work. Action plans work simply because they focus your mind on what needs to be done. Once you have created your action plan, stick it in a prominent position such as your fridge door. This will act as a reminder of the work that you need to do in order to prepare properly for selection. Your action plan might look something like this:

My weekly action plan for preparing for London Underground Train Driver selection

Monday	Tuesday	Wednesday	Thursday	Friday
Research into the organisation I am applying for. Includes reading recruitment literature and visiting websites.	60 minute Interview preparation including preparing my responses to questions.	Obtain application form and read recruitment literature and application form guidance notes.	Research into the organisation I am applying for. Includes reading recruitment literature and visiting websites.	60 minute mock interview with a friend or relative.
60 minutes preparation on Mechanical Comprehension tests and Checking Tests.	30 minute Dot Concentration Tests preparation.	45 minute fast reaction preparation using 'Bop it' toy.	60 minutes preparation on Mechanical Comprehension tests and Checking Tests.	30 minute Dot Concentration Tests preparation.
20 minute jog or brisk walk.	30 minutes gym work.	20 minutes reading about the role of a London Underground Train Driver..	20 minute jog or brisk walk.	30 minutes gym work.

Note: Saturday and Sunday, rest days.

The above sample action plan is just a simple example of what you may wish to include. Your action plan will very much depend on your strengths and weaknesses. After reading this guide, decide which areas you need to work on and then add them to your action plan. Areas that you may wish to include in your action plan could be:

- Researching the role of a London Underground Train Driver.

- Researching the training that you will undergo as a Trainee Driver.

- Researching the organisation that you are applying for and the Transport for London website.

- Dedicating time to completing the application form and reading the guidance notes.

- Carrying out practice tests that are similar to the ones required at the assessment centre.

- Light fitness work in order to keep up your concentration levels.

- Interview preparation including carrying out a mock interview.

You will note that throughout the duration of this guide I make continued reference to 'preparation'. During my career I have been successful at over 95% of the interviews and assessments that I've attended. The reason for this is because I always embark on a period of focused preparation, and I always aim to improve on my weak areas. Follow this simple process and you too can enjoy the same levels of success that I have enjoyed.

Finally, it is very important that you believe in your own abilities. It does not matter if you have no qualifications. It does not matter if you have no knowledge yet of the role of a London Underground Train Driver. What does matter is self belief, self discipline and a genuine desire to improve and become successful.

Enjoy reading the guide and then set out on a period of intense preparation!

Best wishes,

Richard McMunn

Richard McMunn

The London Underground, or Tube, is an iconic symbol of the city, much the same as the New York Subway is. The Underground has been in operation for a very long time, and serves to help residents, visitors and businesspeople get around the city, without fighting the congestion on the surface streets.

The London Underground contains 270 stations and serves approximately 1.265 billion people on an annual basis. The system actually started in 1863, though it has grown immensely since that time, and has become an integral part of London's transportation network.

For those seeking a rewarding career, the choice to become a London Underground train driver can be a remarkable one. The job offers plenty of stability, excellent earning potential and numerous other benefits. How do you go about getting started? What sort of career path can you look forward to? What sort of education is required to enter this field? This book will give you all the information you need to know about embarking on a rewarding career as a train driver on the London Underground. You will learn more about the history of this iconic, vital transportation system, how to get the selection process started and even how to pass the interview for the job.

The history of the London Underground is one of gradual changes, as the system evolved from its simple beginnings into the modern transport system, which has become so important to Londoners. In fact, you might even call the beginning of this monolithic system "inauspicious".

A NEED FOR CHANGE

Before we delve into the history of the Underground, it is important to understand why such a system was even invented. Since pre-Roman Britain, London has been a constant hub of activity. In the first half of the 1800s, train travel boomed, to the extent that the period itself was nicknamed 'the Railway Mania'. This period saw explosive growth of railways all over the world. In Britain, there were numerous train lines that led into London, but many of these terminated relatively far from the city centre. This made it difficult for some passengers to reach their destination.

During the 1830s, the need for alterations to the current train terminus system was noted. There were many different plans proposed during this period, but the majority were never put into practice, and subsequently abandoned. The plan that was eventually adopted was to run a broad-gauge line from Paddington Station on the Great Western Railway toward the city. Paddington was, at the time, the furthest station from the city, and the completion of new stations only served to make the situation worse. The plan was adopted by the GWR, as well as vouched for by the Great Northern Railway (GNR). The entire plan was adopted as the Metropolitan Railway on the 7th of August, 1854.

PROBLEMS IN THE EARLY YEARS

Of course, the best-laid plans can often come to nothing. For a long time, it seemed that the Metropolitan Railway would be one of those, as no progress was made for several years after the formal adoption of the plan. This was due to the fact that there was little or no funding available. Without funding to pay the workers, there was simply no way to build the railway. In 1858, Charles Pearson (the driving force behind construction of the railway) announced that the system would provide working class people with affordable, simple transportation from the outlying areas into the heart of the city for work. After this announcement, funding became available and construction continued.

Construction of the system advanced relatively quickly after that point, although there were still many problems to overcome. The line from Paddington to King's Cross was completed as a cut and cover style, while the line after that point was simply open cut. Throughout the process, excavations collapsed, causing a tremendous amount of additional work. Later, the Fleet Ditch Sewer actually burst and flooded the entire system with sewage. When the Board of Trade inspected the system, it declared that the owners needed to make additional changes.

After all of the changes, problems and hurdles, the line finally opened in January of 1863. The first day, more than 40,000 passengers were carried. This set the tone for the rest of the development. During the first year, the MetR faced another problem when GWR backed out of its decision to operate the line. The MetR turned to GNR and LNW for locomotives, though, and GWR eventually began running a handful of trains again.

It also took some time for the system to settle on fares. Early on, the line charged 3d per return fare. Later, though, this fare was reduced to a single penny per train. With affordable transport fees, the MetR became an enormous hit. In fact, by 1880, it was carrying 40 million passengers per year to and from the city and the Inner Circle was under construction.

ADDITIONAL GROWTH COMES TO TOWN

By 1871, the MetR line was in deep financial trouble, but it continued to serve the portion of the city's Inner Circle that had been completed, in conjunction with the Metropolitan District Railway. It was in 1884 that the MDR finally opened the City Lines and Extensions. This completed the Inner Circle and passengers were able to ride the District trains throughout the southern half, or the MetR trains through the northern half of the circle.

DEEP TUBES – THE BEGINNING

Until the development of the deep tubes, the entire system was either open cuts or cut and cover. However, in the 1890s, the first successful deep tube line was opened to the public. This ran from King William Street to Stockwell. Technically, the first deep tube system was located beneath the River Thames, but it was not successful and was closed shortly after opening.

However, the story was very different with the City and South London Railway (the one linking King William Street to Stockwell). While the system was not particularly comfortable or spacious, it was popular. The success of this line spurred a host of other plans for similar lines, many of which were approved. However, a lack of funding kept almost all of them from even the beginning stages of construction.

By the end of the decade, only two new tube lines had come into existence. These were the Waterloo and City Railway, which opened in 1898, and the Central London Railway, which opened in 1900. The Waterloo and City Railway operated from Waterloo to Bank Station within the city, and the Central London Railway served what would become the Central Line in modern times.

In 1902, Charles Yerkes, an American with experience operating electric trains and trams in the city of Chicago, purchased several lines and built a power station to supply electricity to deep trains. The same year, he launched the Underground Electric Railways Company of London (UERL). UERL soon bought out and controlled many of the once independent companies, with the exception being MetR, W&CR and the GN&CR lines. However, things were about to change.

THE BIRTH OF THE UNDERGROUND

While UERL had been making headway by using the name Underground to promote the many lines under its control, a recognisable modern Underground system had to wait for the aftermath of WWI to evolve. It was during this time that Parliament recommended that the city of London have a single traffic authority. This was enacted to reduce high fairs and unfair competition, and to ease the burden on the city's passengers. The post of Minister of Transport was created in 1919.

The London Passenger Transport Board (LT) was created during this time, and was actually an amalgamation of MetR, the Underground Group and the city's bus and tramlines, as well. The new board set several plans in motion for expansion and modification of the city's subway system. The entire system saw new growth, with lines being extended, and new stations being designed and built. This lasted until the outbreak of WW2, which caused it to halt.

THE UNDERGROUND IN WWII

While the Underground did not play a major role in any war time offence, or in troop movement, it did play an important defensive role for the city during WW2. Many of the stations began to be used as air-raid shelters, particularly during The Blitz. While there were some instances where considerable loss of life occurred, the stations worked very well for this purpose, as most of them were protected by the earth from bombs dropped by Nazi warplanes.

Another interesting use of the system was as an aircraft manufacturing station, while another portion was used as a control point for anti-aircraft efforts. Winston Churchill also used the Down Street Station for his war meetings, at least until the Cabinet War Rooms were completed.

In all, there was nothing in the way of growth or expansion during the years of WWII. However, the Underground still played an essential role in the lives of Londoners.

AFTER WWII

Following WW2, the Underground began to take on a more modern appearance. However, first it had to suffer through the mismanagement brought about by nationalisation and the British Transport Commission. The BTC was given control over the Underground and over the city's bus and tramlines on the surface. Nevertheless, the BTC did oversee the final stages of electrification of the Underground. The last steam-powered passenger trains were removed from the lines in 1961, though some remained in use for engineering purposes on surface lines until 1971.

In 1963, the BTC was demolished, and London Transport was put under control of a separate board. Under this board, growth once again began, with the completion of the Victoria Line. This was the first line to use automatic train operation for the entirety of its route. The Jubilee Line opened in 1979, and has seen considerable development and redevelopment since that time, with extensions, route changes and more.

In 1984, the LRT (London Regional Transport) came into being, and London Underground Limited (LUL) was created in 1985. These were both part of the modernisation of the system and a reduction in subsidies from taxpayers and ratepayers. However, in 2000, the LRT was removed and the TfL took over control of London Underground. TfL (Transport for London) also controls the city's bus lines, tram lines and even has control over some airports within the city, as well. Today, the entire setup is considered a PPP, or Public-Private Partnership. Here, the entire infrastructure of the network, as well as the "rolling stock," is maintained by two private companies. However, London Underground Limited (LUL) remains a publicly owned company controlled by Transport for London.

SETBACKS AND CHANGES

After the Thatcher government enacted numerous changes designed to save money and reduce payroll, significant problems occurred. While the changes certainly did help to boost the profitability of the London Underground, and had numerous supporters, they also had several detrimental effects.

The King's Cross St Pancras fire of 1987, which killed 31 people in the station, seemed to be a direct result of staff cuts, combined with outdated equipment and design. While smoking was banned in these stations, authorities deem it most likely that a passenger discarded a lit match. This match landed on the track, which was filthy with debris and oil. The debris caught fire, which quickly spread to the escalator. In a modern application, this would not have been terrible. However, the escalator was built just after WW2, and the sides were made of wood. This wood was old and dry, and acted like kindling for the fire, which quickly consumed the escalator and spread throughout the station causing enormous amounts of damage.

In the aftermath of the tragedy, it was revealed that the number of cleaning staff at the station had been reduced from 14, to just 2 people. This was why the track was in such poor condition. The immediate reaction to the disaster was to demolish and replace all of the wooden escalators present on the Underground, and to hire new staff members to clean and sanitise station premises.

THE CURRENT ERA

Today the current London Underground remains an essential part of the city's infrastructure. However, it does face some unique challenges in the times ahead. How the network meets these challenges will largely affect how vital it remains to Londoners. What are these concerns?

Ventilation – One of the major concerns here is adequate ventilation. Currently, the only ventilation shafts for the underground network were built in the Victorian era, and are insufficient for providing adequate ventilation for the network.

The only major source of air movement is the piston effect of trains passing through tunnels and by platforms. This movement helps ensure that fresh air is somewhat evenly distributed. However, it is not sufficient for providing large quantities of fresh air or of controlling temperatures.

Ongoing experiments with the system are being attempted, to help provide better ventilation for the tunnels and even air conditioning for the trains, themselves.

Flooding – Flooding is a problem that has actually grown in recent years. As more and more businesses in the city that use large quantities of water shut down, that water builds in the underground network. In addition, the increasing amount of rain the city has been receiving adds to the problem. London's water levels have been consistently rising since the 1960s. Currently, London Underground has to pump 30 million litres of water out of the system every single day.

Presently, London Underground is comprised of eleven different lines. These are the Bakerloo Line (Brown); Central Line (Red); Circle Line (Yellow); District Line (Green); Hammersmith and City Line (Pink); Jubilee Line (Silver); Metropolitan Line (Dark Magenta); Northern Line (Black); Piccadilly Line (Dark Blue); Victoria Line (Light Blue); Waterloo and City Line (Turquoise).

The network also operates 270 different train stations, and 14 of these are located outside of Greater London. Those outside the greater metro area include five that are actually outside the M25. There are six boroughs in the city that are not served by any Underground station.

THE FUTURE OF THE UNDERGROUND

London Underground continues to grow. There are numerous plans for improvements and expansions in the future. For instance, automatic train operation is scheduled for the mid 2020's, and by 2016 TFL is aiming to have trebled the number of air conditioned trains in their service. This will cover around 40% of the network.

The Bakerloo Line might be extended, as well, if the Mayor's plans come to fruition, and the Crossrail plan is set to debut in 2017, though it will not actually be part of London Underground. However, the Chelsea-Hackney Line slated for construction after the Crossrail plan will most likely be part of London Underground, and will provide a line going from the northeast to the south of the city.

A STUDY OF LONDON UNDERGROUND ROLLING STOCK

No discussion of London Underground would be complete without at least a brief mention of the system's rolling stock, or trains. You will find that there are quite a few different types of trains used on a regular basis, as both Deep Tube trains and subsurface trains. Both types are different, due to the size differences in the tunnels and the cut and cover system for subsurface trains.

Underground trains are a popular topic of study for historians and for those who enjoy modern technology. It is highly worthwhile, as a train driver, to research the past development of British transport and the type of trains that have previously been used.

THE EARLY DAYS

During the early days of the network, trains were all powered by steam. These were a special class of steam locomotive, designed specifically to run within the tunnel environment. Several different types were developed, beginning in 1864 with the A Class. The last year that steam locomotives were produced for this purpose was in 1924, with the K Class. However, steam locomotives remained in use for quite some time after this point, and were not fully removed from service until 1971.

Steam locomotives had the longest running role in the network, largely due to the slow advance of technology. However, electric trains did debut early on, but the effort to electrify the entire system was greatly hampered by the war. During both WWI and WWII, no significant advancements were made with London Underground, and steam locomotives continued to be the primary trains in use.

THE NEXT TRAINS

The next type of train to debut within London Underground was the electric locomotive. These actually began to be used in 1880, with the opening of the City and South London Railway, which was the first deep-level tube of the network. Electric trains were a great improvement over steam locomotives, simply because they did not require coal to run, and produced no exhaust. These trains were enormously popular with passengers, and had a very long run in the system. However, these were done away with by 1962, though some examples can still be found in museums.

CURRENT ROLLING STOCK

The current rolling stock, both Deep Tube and Subsurface, is made up of battery-electric trains. These are considerably different from even the older electric trains, not to mention the steam locomotives of days gone by.

Battery-electric trains have the capability to run on the electric current flowing through the track, but also have a battery bank designed to provide electric power should there be a problem with the line. You might be more familiar with these trains as battery locomotives, or by their nickname, tunnelrats.

Currently, the oldest design still in service dates back to 1964. The L20 – L32 trains were built by Metro Cammell and remain in use to this day.

Newer designs have also debuted, and there will be new rolling stock in coming years. For instance, S Stock are expected to replace all of their trains on the District Line, by 2017. New trains will be air conditioned, and will use regenerative brakes. Deep Tube are also currently in the designing stage for capacity increases, and automated trains. By the end of 2015, TFL are aiming to have 18 new trains available for the Jubilee line, and 50 for the Northern line.

CHAPTER 2

HOW TO APPLY TO BECOME A LONDON UNDERGROUND TRAIN DRIVER

As you can see from the previous section, London Underground has a long, rich history. It is an essential element of the city, and is still growing. You can be a part of this network by becoming a London Underground train driver. But how do you go about applying? What should you know about the process? This chapter will discuss how to begin your journey as a train driver, as well as other information that will be important to future applicants.

INFORMATION ABOUT BEING A LONDON UNDERGROUND TRAIN DRIVER

Before we leap into how to start the application process, you should know a bit more about this career option. For instance, what is the earning potential? What sort of advancement potential is there? How long is the average career as a train driver with London Underground? Let us take a look at some of these areas and how they apply to you.

EARNING POTENTIAL

Of course, the salary that you will earn is going to be one of your top priorities. Thankfully, train drivers can earn a decent salary, and can do so in a relatively short period of time. However, you will start out as a trainee driver, with a salary somewhere around £20, 000 to £30,000 per year. After completing your training and moving up to a full driver position, you can expect to earn far more – almost double, in fact.

Most train drivers earn around £35,000 per year, although very qualified, highly experienced drivers can earn in excess of this. Drivers for Eurostar can earn considerably more than their city based counterparts. Your subsidies on the city's transportation network also form a part of your compensation package.

RESPONSIBILITIES

Understanding the responsibilities of a train driver is very important. There are many different things for which a driver is responsible, and they are all vital. What might you be expected to do? You will have to ensure that the train is in good working order before leaving. You will also have to make sure that any freight is loaded correctly (a rarity with London Underground). Finally, you will have to learn the route which you will follow, and coordinate with the control centre.

During the course of a trip, you will have to learn about delays and problems ahead, plan for these and make your passengers aware of them, as well. You will also need to understand current track conditions and weather conditions, as well as how these will affect travel. You will need to follow signals and safety regulations at all times, keep the train under control and at the correct speed, and make announcements to passengers.

Other responsibilities of drivers include opening automatic doors at stations, understanding emergency procedures, stopping the train at the correct locations, adhering to the correct schedule, and more. You will need to alert your relief driver to any problems, accidents or hazards, keep a record of any problems encountered, record delays that affect service and alert the control centre to hazards you might encounter on your route.

QUALIFICATIONS

Becoming a London Underground train driver requires that you have numerous qualifications. What are these? Most are preliminary qualifications prior to any specific training regimen required to drive a train. Here is a list of qualifications that you will need to have.

First, you need to be at least 21 years of age to start training to be a train driver with any entity other than London Underground. In addition, you will need to have good GCSE grades to show that you have a good standard of education. While there are really no formal education requirements to enter this field, having A Level and A1 Level grades will appeal to the organisation.

You will also need to present your formal application to the company (which will be covered in this chapter), and then attend a formal training centre. Here, you will sit for several aptitude tests, which will assess your skills, knowledge and proficiency in many different areas. You will also need to pass a physical examination, an eyesight examination and drug tests.

THE TRAINING PROCESS

In general, becoming a London Underground train driver will require that you undergo 22 weeks of training. However, if you opt to train outside of London Underground, you might have to sit through 48 weeks of training. London Underground has some of the lowest training requirements in the industry for potential drivers.

Your training will be multifaceted, and will cover hands-on driver training with an instructor, driving theory and safety training. You will have to complete a Personal Track Safety Certificate, as well as an NVQ Level 2 in Rail Transport Operations (Driving) before your training is complete. You will also need to be familiar with the rules and guidelines of working on the railroad.

THE SKILLS REQUIRED

In addition to training and other qualifications, you will find that train drivers need a very defined set of skills. These include the following:

Good Mechanical Knowledge – Knowledge of mechanics is a "must" for train drivers. Not only will you need to spot potential mechanical problems, but there might be times when you are called upon to fix those problems yourself, rather than waiting for an engineer to do it.

Good Hand-Eye Coordination – Having good hand-eye coordination is incredibly important for train drivers. As you will be driving a very heavy vehicle, filled with passengers, you will need to be able to react to hazards, track obstructions and other conditions instantly. Handling a train can be a very intense experience, and this quality makes it easier.

Concentration – Being a train driver will require that you have the ability to hold your concentration and focus for long periods of time. You must be able to drive the train while concentrating on the task at hand for the entire length of the route.

Physical Stamina – While driving a train is not the most physical job in the world, you will find having good stamina helps you in the role. The act of driving and concentrating for long periods of time can cause fatigue, and therefore it is useful if you are in healthy condition.

Good Communication Skills – You must be a good communicator. Not only will you have to communicate over the PA system of the train, but you will also have to communicate with the control centre, with other personnel and even with passengers in a face-to-face setting. Solid communication skills are vital here.

Dealing with the Public – As mentioned above, you will have to deal with the public on a regular basis. Often, these passengers will be harried, stressed, aggravated or angry.

You will have to deal with them all equably, and offer good customer service to them.

Good Reaction Times – Driving a train means that there will be times when you have to react swiftly. This might involve reacting to an emergency situation on the train, or a hazard on the tracks. You need to ensure that you have good reaction times and decision making to be successful as a train driver.

Good Memory – Often, you will have to rely on your memory during this job. Whether it is navigating a particular route, recalling details for the control centre or something else entirely, you will need to have a good memory to be a success driving trains for London Underground.

Flexibility – You need to have a flexible schedule to enjoy working as a train driver. Most often, you will find that this is shift work, and you will be put on a rotating schedule that covers all available shifts. This distributes the workload evenly amongst drivers, even though you might prefer having a set schedule.

Health and Safety Regulations/Emergency Procedures – Most of these will be taught to you during training. However, you need to make sure that you are fully aware of health and safety regulations, as well as how to react in emergency situations. You will be responsible for the lives of your passengers, so this knowledge is essential.

Remaining Calm Under Pressure – While driving a train is not the most stressful position in the world, it does have pressure. You will be dealing with the public, with the control centre, with other personnel and with track issues all at the same time. This can lead to a stressful situation. You need to be able to remain calm under pressure to handle these situations correctly.

Reliability – London Underground runs on a tight schedule. Even the smallest things can throw that schedule off. Your level of reliability will help ensure that your train runs on time, that your passengers are safe and more. A reliable driver is the best kind, and therefore the most likely to succeed within the role.

WORKING CONDITIONS IN THE UNDERGROUND

London Underground has very different working conditions from train driving positions with surface railways. Shift work will certainly be part of your working conditions and should be accepted from the outset. In addition, you will find that temperature extremes can be great, particularly during the winter and summer. Wintertime can be very cold, while the heat during the summer can be considerable. You will be required to wear a uniform at all times.

As a final note, you will need to be comfortable with being alone much of the time. While your train might be filled with passengers, your cab will usually be just for you. You might go an entire route without seeing another person, and speaking only over the PA or the radio to the control centre.

THE FUTURE OF THE CAREER

Where can you go from this position? What are your options for moving up if you tire of driving for London Underground? Obviously, you do not want to enter a job where there are no opportunities to progress within the field. Thankfully, there are several options if you wish to continue your career within the industry.

Many people go on to become trainers and teachers – you might work for London Underground in this capacity, or you might choose to work with a private training company. You might also choose to become a driver for another railway, or even become a Eurostar driver, which is often considered the pinnacle of the career. Regardless, there are quite a few options for you if you wish to move up and branch out.

Besides London Underground, there are many other employers out there for whom you might choose to work. These include the following:

- Eurostar

- Freight companies

- Engineering supply companies

- Metro companies

- Light rail companies

THE APPLICATION – HOW, WHERE AND WHY

The key to gaining employment is the London Underground application. You can apply for jobs through numerous options, though online applications have become very popular. You can also apply for London Underground jobs through TfL (http://www.TfL.gov.uk). Regardless, you will need to complete the application. This can be trickier than you might think.

The first order of business is to read the entire application before filling anything out. You might find different requirements, such as using black ink only or writing in block capital letters. You need to adhere to these requirements or your application will likely be thrown in the bin.

Once you have read the entire application and all associated forms, you can begin filling them out. However, you need to ensure that you fill everything out completely. Write in your competencies, your education, your background and all other information that the application requests. Once you are finished, you will need to send in your application to the specified office. If you use an online application, you will simply need to hit "send" to start the process off.

In addition to the TfL website, you can search for train driver jobs and other rail jobs with the following websites:

- JustRail – www.JustRail.net

- Calco – www.Calco.co.uk

- WorkGateways – www.WorkGateways.com

On **page 24** we have provided you with all the details you will need to know, whilst filling in your application.

TFL also offers both graduate and apprenticeship schemes for aspiring employees. As a graduate, you would have access to over 30 different options, so there are plenty of choices to suit your interests. You would also gain a free Oyster card, receive private medical benefits and up to 75% discount on future rail travel. Likewise, there are a diverse range of apprenticeship schemes available. The application process is largely the same for both, and similar to the application process for non-graduate/apprentice employees. Over the new few pages, we will show you how to go about applying.

STARTING OUT IN ANOTHER POSITION

While it might not be your preferred route, you might just find that you have to start out in a different position from driver. Often, you will find that London Underground does not hire drivers from the public pool, but offers the jobs in-house first. If those positions are not able to be filled by existing staff, then they will be advertised to the public. Therefore, you might find that starting out as station staff and then moving to a driver position is the best option for your needs. Often, you can sign on as a member of the station staff, and move up in only a matter of months. London Underground makes it quite simple for existing staff to move to being a driver, and even provide what are called Training Days to help their employees learn new skills required to be more successful within the organisation.

Another reason to consider this route, is because of the low number of driver positions offered at any one time. There are only so many positions to go around, and therefore when a job is advertised, the response is often overwhelming. If you are able to get a job working at a station, the process will be much easier, and will ensure that you are generating income whilst you wait for a position to become available. Existing employees have a much better chance of getting the position than those working outside the rail industry.

If you are an existing employee, your chances of getting that coveted position are greater than if you were an anonymous applicant off the street.

PREPARING TO COMPLETE THE APPLICATION FORM

Most of the sections on the application form are relatively straightforward to complete. However, there are a number of very important sections which will require your utmost attention if you wish to be successful. First, read the following tips and advice on completing your application form:

Read everything first
This applies to both the application form, the accompanying literature (if any) and the TfL website. You will need to understand a little bit about the company first before you can successfully complete the application form. You should also study the job description, person specification and the accompanying recruitment guidance notes.

Correct ink colour
Unless you are submitting an online application make sure you read any requirements that relate to ink colour or capital letters etc. The TfL Recruitment Office will receive hundreds of applications for every job advertised and the initial sift will look at minor errors such as these. If you cannot follow simple instructions such as the correct ink colour then there is not much chance you'll be able to operate a train safely. Read everything carefully and follow all of the instructions.

Complete a rough draft first
The first time around you are more than likely to make some mistakes. I advise that you photocopy the application form first (unless you are completing an online version) and complete a rough draft first. This will give you the opportunity to practice. Then, once you have finished your application, take a copy of it so that you can refer to it before you attend the interview. The panel will most certainly refer to your application form during the interview.

As has been mentioned, completing your application form correctly is an essential ingredient to presenting the most favourable image possible. You will discover that there are numerous areas of concern on the application – this chapter will walk you through filling it out correctly, before submitting it to the company.

Below, you will find the form broken down into separate sections. Each of these sections is important in its own right, and should be considered carefully prior to filling out the application. Towards the end of this chapter, I have provided you with a number of sample application form questions and responses to assist you in your preparation.

ADVICE ON COMPLETING THE DIFFERENT SECTIONS

Your Personal Information

Make sure that you fill out all of your personal information on the application, including your name, your date of birth, your address, telephone number, cellular phone number and email address (if applicable). You should also make it clear what your sex is – a simple Mr. or Mrs. before your name will do the trick here.

The number of people who fail to put down all of their personal information is startling. You should make certain that this section is as complete as possible. Not only does it ensure that the hirer has the information needed to contact you when your application is accepted, but it shows that you are thorough and detail-oriented.

Your Education Information

The lack of a formal education requirement for London Underground train drivers has been mentioned several times thus far. Does that mean your education information is not important? Quite the reverse, actually – make sure that you do list your education. However, you need to do this in the right order.

You should list any higher education completed first – your A Levels and A1 Levels. You should also list any degrees earned, and any course of study that might be of interest to the hirer. For instance, completing a business course, an engineering course, transportation work and other education will make you a more qualified candidate in their eyes.

After your highest education, list your GCSE grades. However, because these are so basic, you should not list every single pass you received, unless you have no other education. You should also ensure that you list any qualifications you might have, such as H&S, C25 or D32, as this makes you a more qualified job candidate and the information is of interest to the hirer.

Previous Employment
This is another area of incredible importance. You need to ensure that you show a full background of employment, whether that is a history of part-time jobs or fulltime employment. Employers look unfavourably on times when you were unemployed, so make sure you clarify any periods of unemployment longer than a couple of weeks. List the reason that you were not employed, any overriding situations that might have made working impossible and other information here.

When listing your previous employment experience, start with your current or most recent employer. Work backwards from this point for the time period specified on the application. Generally, you will find that five years is sufficient, though more can often be included, particularly if you spent a considerable amount of time with one company.

Make sure that you include all pertinent information for each employer. You will need the employer's name, address, telephone number, the name of your supervisor and more. In addition, include the dates you were employed, your job duties, accomplishments on the job, and your position. Highlight any experience, skills or knowledge that might be of interest to the hirer here, such as working with the public, jobs where safety was paramount or shift work.

Listing Your Interests

What possible use could your personal interests serve on your application? Actually, they can be very valuable. Not only do they serve to highlight the fact that you are a well-rounded person, but they also serve to make you stand out from others. Do not go overboard with your interests, but make sure that you list some of them.

In particular, you want to list any interests that relate directly to the job – perhaps you are a railroad enthusiast, or maybe you enjoy working with computers. As a note, only list interests that show you as a calm, rational individual capable of making well-reasoned decisions.

Skills, Skills, Skills

In addition to the skills you have doubtless learned on other jobs (and listed appropriately), you need to list other skills that you have. Are you computer literate? Can you use common computer office software like MS Word or MS Excel? You might also choose to list other skills that you have learned – you might have first aid certification, or taken lifesaving courses previously. List these, as they make you a more valuable asset to the company.

You should also list any foreign languages in which you are fluent, because this will serve you well as a train driver. Almost any secondary skill can be a valuable addition to your application in this section, so long as it can be translated into an advantage for a train driver.

Travel Capabilities

If you have a vehicle and are able to make any shift available, list this. If you live near a particular train depot, then list this information as well. In addition, if you are willing to relocate for the job, provide this information on your application.

London Underground (and other TOCs) prefers to have employees located within a specific distance of terminals, as well as having employees with their own transportation. These two assets alone can be enough to differentiate your application from 75% of those that are turned in. You should also research whether there is a maximum distance from the terminal required, before you turn in your application form.

Previous Experience as a Train Driver
Do you have previous experience as a train driver? If so, then you are an excellent candidate for employment with London Underground if they have positions open. The company always prefers to hire job candidates with experience whenever possible, though this is not a requirement. The training centre is well equipped to help teach new recruits all that is necessary to perform their job duties. However, if you are already a train driver, then you will need to follow some special steps that do not apply to other job applicants. What are these steps?

The first thing that you need to do is fill out your Transfer of Safety-Critical Information form. You will find an example in the RGS Approved Code of Practice – Train Driving. Your existing employer is required to provide you with this information, as it is evidence of your safety record on the job. This information is an essential step in obtaining employment with London Underground. You will also need to write down your current route and traction knowledge, as well as any other relevant information, such as qualifications like a C25 or D32, experience as an instructor or a supervisor and more. All of this helps the company determine your value to them and ensure that you are the right candidate for the position.

Another thing that you should state is that you have already passed all the assessment tests, the physical and the vision test. This gives you an advantage over other applicants, in that London Underground will not need to spend time or effort testing you in these areas. If you have been a train driver in the past, but are not currently employed as one, you will need to follow some special steps, as well. First, you need to understand that your experience and competencies are only valid for a six-month period after leaving your position. Therefore, if you were a train driver a year ago, your competencies are no longer valid in the eyes of the hirer.

What does this mean? Simply put, you will have to undergo refresher training to some degree, depending on how long you have been out of the industry. The longer you have been out, the more retraining you will require. However, you should also understand that this only works for a period of five years from the point of your departure from the driving position. If it has been longer than five years, London Underground will consider you a new hire and require that you undergo the full battery of training and testing. If possible, you need to have proof of your employment within a train driving position showing how long it has been since you last held the job.

Finally, if you are a train driver from another country, you will have other special requirements. First, you will be required to speak and read English proficiently. You will also find that any qualifications you earned in another country will not transfer to your career in London. You still need to have a Certificate of Competence in order to drive trains for London Underground, or any other railway in the nation. However your foreign qualifications do lend you an advantage in the application process. Because you have experience and you have earned those qualifications, you have an edge over applicants who have no training or previous experience at all to speak of.

Reply Timeframe

Ideally, you will want a very fast response to your application – it is nice to know at least something, whether that is positive or negative. However, the wait time can be quite long – months in some cases. Why is this? You have to remember the number of other applicants who are applying for the job as well.

When London Underground advertises a train driving position, they can very quickly receive several thousand applications. Going through these applications takes a lot of time. You can minimise your wait time by getting your application in as quickly as possible. The sooner your application is received and reviewed, the sooner you will receive a response, or at least a confirmation that the company has received your application.

On the following pages, I have provided you with a number of sample responses to some of the most common types of question. You will find these questions on both London Underground Train Driver Forms, and generic TOC Trainee Train Driver Forms. The 'question and answer' sections on the application form are very important and represent an opportunity for you to show the recruitment staff how good you are. Before each question I have explained what the question means and how best to construct your response to it. Then, I have provided you with a sample response to each question. Please note that these are to be used as a guide only. It is important that you answer the questions on your application form based on your own experiences and knowledge.

SAMPLE QUESTION NUMBER 1

Now that you've read more about the job, please tell us why you're applying for it and what knowledge, experience or skills you have that might be relevant.

The clue in this type of question is to READ about the job you are applying for. The question is asking you to match your knowledge, experience and skills with the job you have applied for. Therefore you need to read the job description before responding. Job descriptions or person specifications usually have both 'essential' and 'desirable' criteria included. Basically you must provide evidence of where you can meet the 'essential' criteria on your application form. Desirable criteria will gain you extra marks but they are not essential.

If TfL, or the organisation you applying to join, have not sent you a copy of the job description, try to obtain a copy of it before completing the form. This will give you an insight into the role that you are applying for. Once you have read the information about the post you will then be able to construct a suitable answer. Try to include any knowledge, skills or experience you may have that relates to the job description. If you have experience or knowledge in health and safety, working in pressurised situations or working in a customer-based environment then you may wish to include these also.

The Train Driver position is one that requires 100% attention at all times, and an ability to learn new skills quickly and accurately. Again, if you have experience of working in these conditions then say so. Now take a look at the following sample response before constructing your own, based on your own skills, knowledge and experience.

SAMPLE RESPONSE TO QUESTION NUMBER 1

I am applying for this post because I am looking for a new and challenging role. I enjoy working in a customer-focused environment and believe I would make an excellent London Underground Train Driver for your company. I am also prepared to relocate if necessary. I understand that the company is changing and moving forward and I believe you would be an exciting company to work for. I also believe I can bring something to the team in terms of commitment, motivation and enthusiasm.

I have worked in a customer-based role for a number of years now and during this time I have developed skills that can be applied to the role of a Train Driver. As well as being a good communicator and possessing excellent practical skills I am also highly safety conscious and understand that this is a very important element of the role. In addition to my 12 years experience in a customer-focused role I worked for 4 years with the Royal Navy. I am therefore a highly disciplined person and a very good team player. I have educational qualifications in English Language, English Literature and Art and I am also coming to the end of studying for a Diploma in Management Studies. I also hold a Health and Safety qualification through IODA in Nottingham. I am a fit and active person who visits the gym/swimming pool three times a week and I also play football for a local Sunday team. I am a very good communicator and learn new skills quickly. I am used to working long and varied hours and I understand that the role requires a high level of flexibility, which I am prepared for. I enjoy working with, and meeting people from all walks of life and I truly value the benefits of a diverse workforce. To summarise, I am a highly professional, caring, trustworthy, friendly and motivated person and I believe I would make an excellent member of your team.

SAMPLE QUESTION NUMBER 2

Please tell us about anything you get up to outside work that gives us a better idea of what you're like as a person and why you might be right for our company. Please give the name of the activity and what it says about you.

This type of question is designed to assess the type of person you are outside of work. This will give the company an idea of how you are likely to perform at work and will tell them if you are fit, healthy and active. When responding to this type of question, make sure you make reference to the job description. What type of duties will you be required to perform and can you match your external activities to them? Being fit and active is always a positive aspect that the recruitment staff will be looking for. If you are active outside of work, then you are also likely to be active at work and achieve your tasks to the required standard. If you have recently achieved any educational or academic qualifications outside of work then it would be a good idea to make reference to these too. Now take a look at the sample response before creating your own based around your own skills, knowledge and experience.

SAMPLE RESPONSE TO QUESTION NUMBER 2

KEEPING FIT - *I attend the gym at least 3 times per week and carry out some light weight work. Whilst at the gym, I usually perform 20 minutes of rowing each time and cover a distance of 5,000 metres. I particularly enjoy swimming and swim 50 lengths, 3 times per week. When I get the opportunity I also like to go walking, this keeps me healthy. Staying fit and healthy means that I am able to maintain a high level of concentration at work and it also helps to keep my enthusiasm and motivation levels high. This shows that I am a dedicated and determined person who is always looking to improve himself.*

SAMPLE RESPONSE TO QUESTION NUMBER 3

During a recent staff meeting I was aware that there were a number of problems between some members of the team. The team wasn't working effectively so we all discussed ways in which we could improve. The actions of the team were starting to have an effect on the team's performance, so I decided to take the initiative to resolve the issue. I facilitated the meeting and asked everybody to share their views and opinions. I listened to each person individually and tried to encourage people to come up with solutions in order to improve the team's effectiveness. A positive point that came from our discussions was that people felt that we didn't hold enough meetings to talk about the problems we all face. It was agreed that with immediate effect we would hold weekly meetings to discuss issues, gather and share information, and look for ways that we could all support each other in our work. Since the meeting the team has moved forward and is now working far more effectively.

SAMPLE QUESTION NUMBER 4

As the role you've applied for means that you'll be dealing with the safety of our customers and the delivery of our operation, we would like to hear examples of how you have developed your abilities to improve yourself.

Having the ability to constantly review your own performance and take steps to improve is an important aspect of everyday life. This is particularly relevant in the workplace and, with a role that requires high safety standards and adherence, this is very much the case.

When responding to this type of question, try to think of an example or examples where you have improved yourself. This may be through a training course or educational qualification(s). You must ensure that you provide good examples to this type of question as the TfL recruitment staff want to see that you have the ability to pass the initial training course and absorb new skills relatively easily. Now take a look at the following sample response before creating your own.

SAMPLE RESPONSE TO QUESTION NUMBER 4

In order to carry out my duties in my current role effectively, I felt that I needed more management skills. I decided to pay for, and embark on, a Diploma Course in Management. I am coming to the end of the course and have found it a useful tool for improving my skills. I am always looking for new ways to improve my skills and knowledge so that I can perform better both in a professional and personal capacity. I also believe it is important to keep fully up-to-date and familiar with company health and safety policies and, every week, I read the company safety log to ensure I am aware of any changes or amendments to policy. The safety of our customers and clients is paramount and I have developed many skills in this area that I believe would be an asset to the role of London Underground Train Driver with your company.

SAMPLE QUESTION NUMBER 5

As the role you've applied for means that you'll be dealing with the safety of our customers and the delivery of our operation, we would like to hear examples of how you have played a positive role as a team member or leader.

Having the ability to work as an effective team member is important in any organisation and the Transport for London are no exception. The organisation will be made up of many different people, all of whom have an important role to perform. Therefore, it is essential that you have had some experience of working in a team environment, either as a team member or team leader. Try to think of an occasion when you have been part of a team or have even been the leader of a team. When responding to questions of this nature, think of a scenario where you worked as part of the team to achieve a task or solve a problem. Now take a look at the sample response, before using a blank sheet of paper to construct your own.

SAMPLE RESPONSE TO QUESTION NUMBER 5

In my current role, I am responsible for the safety of my team and for ensuring that any health and safety incidents are reported in line with company regulations. I am also involved in coaching and mentoring my team and providing them with feedback, often helping them to improve. I currently lead a team of 18 staff and I am required to ensure the team operates effectively in terms of management, health and safety, and training. Following any incident that relates to health and safety I always fully brief each member of the team to ensure that I have done everything in my power to prevent an incident occurring again.

SAMPLE QUESTION NUMBER 6

As the role you've applied for means that you'll be dealing with the safety of our customers and the delivery of our operation, we would like to hear examples of how you have had to work under pressure.

If you are successful in becoming a London Underground Train Driver, you will often encounter occasions when you are under pressure. Maybe you will experience technical difficulties whilst on the train or the air conditioning will fail. You will undoubtedly be presented with scenarios and situations where you have to remain calm and focused and this question is designed to assess your ability to do just that. Try to think of a scenario where you have worked under pressure but still achieved the task or goal.

Take a look at the following sample response before using a blank sheet of paper to construct your own response based on your own experiences.

SAMPLE RESPONSE TO QUESTION NUMBER 6

In my current role as customer service manager I am required to work under pressure on a daily basis. Recently, I was presented with a situation where two members of staff had gone sick leaving me with only three other staff members to manage the shop during a busy Saturday.

During the morning we were due to take a stock delivery which meant that I had to perform many tasks without taking a break. During the day I dealt with two customer complaints, took delivery of the stock, served customers whilst others took their break and also dealt the fire alarm going off. I am often required to perform under pressure and thrive in such conditions. I always adapt well to situations like these and ensure that I still maintain a high level of professionalism at all times.

SAMPLE RESPONSE TO QUESTION NUMBER 7

Whilst working in my current position as a sales person, I was the duty manager for the day as my manager had gone home sick. It was the week before Christmas, and the shop was extremely busy. During the day, the fire alarm went off. In accordance with company policy, I asked everybody to evacuate the shop. The normal manager usually lets customers stay in the shop whilst he finds out if it's a false alarm. This was a very difficult situation. The shop was busy and nobody wanted to leave, my shop assistants disagreed with my decision to evacuate the premises, and some of the customers currently in the changing rooms were extremely unhappy. Several of them threatened to report me to head office. However, I was determined to evacuate everyone from the shop, for safety reasons, and did not allow anybody to deter me from my aim. The safety of both customers and staff was at the forefront of my mind. I persisted with my actions, removed everyone from the shop and called the Fire Service. When they arrived, they informed me that there had been a small fire at the rear of the shop, and that the actions I had taken were the right ones. Nobody was hurt as a result of the incident.

FINAL TIPS FOR CREATING A SUCCESSFUL APPLICATION FORM

- Read the form carefully before starting to complete it. Also be sure to read all of the accompanying guidance notes, person specification and job description.

- Follow all instructions carefully. Your form can be rejected for failing to follow simple instructions.

- If you are completing a handwritten version of the form make sure your handwriting is neat, legible, concise and grammatically correct. You will lose marks for incorrect spelling!

- Before you submit the form, get somebody to check it over for you.

- Provide examples of where you have gained experience(s) that match the job description. For example, safety is an extremely important element of the role.

- Once you have completed the form make sure you make a photocopy of it. You will be asked questions that relate to your responses during the interview.

- Send the form via recorded delivery. I have known of many application forms to go missing in the post.

SITUATIONAL STRENGTH TESTS

After you have completed your application form, you may be required to take a Situational Strength Test. This is a test that is designed to display your ability to respond to certain situations, and will highlight whether you have the decision making skills required to work for them. The questions will be in scenario based multiple choice format. You don't necessarily have to worked for London Underground to answer them, but they should give you some insight into particular aspects of the job. Always answer honestly, rather than simply choosing what you think is the correct response.

CHAPTER 3

UNDERSTANDING THE SELECTION PROCESS FOR LONDON UNDERGROUND TRAIN DRIVERS

Obviously, not all applicants will be selected to become train drivers. There are simply not enough positions for this. In addition, not everyone is a good candidate for the position. How does the selection process work? What are the essential elements to know, in order to maximise your chances of being accepted? This chapter will explore the process of selection. It is important to understand these areas before you even fill out your application.

YOUR APPLICATION

The first thing that the company will see of you will be your application (or CV). Therefore, you need to ensure that you make the best possible impression with your application. The first rule is, as mentioned earlier, to fill it out as completely as possible. The second rule is to ensure that it is as neat and legible as possible. Coffee rings from your mug, sloppy handwriting and unreadable spelling are all things that will reduce the efficacy of your application.

You also need to ensure that you include a cover letter with your application, as this makes it seem much more professional and can give you an added edge when seeking employment. As a final note, make sure that the application highlights your strengths and specialties. If you have previous experience in the realm of public transport, make sure that you highlight this. If you have experience dealing with the public, with high-pressure situations or with considerable responsibility, make sure that you highlight it.

YOUR EDUCATION

Simply put, there is no formal education required to become a train driver. However, that does not mean that education is not important. You should make sure that your educational achievements are listed, as good grades indicate dedication on your part.

List all of your GCSE grades, as well as any A Level or A1 Level grades you have. This will show that you are a dedicated person, that you are willing to study and that you have a commitment to succeeding.

THE ASSESSMENT CENTRE

After you have completed the application and it has met with approval, you will be invited to attend the assessment centre. Here, you will undergo several types of tests. These tests are designed to determine your skills, proficiencies and weaknesses. While you should not fear them, they are an enormous part of the selection process. If you do not pass these tests, then you cannot become a train driver – it is as simple as that.

Obviously, this means that you will have to know quite a bit more about the assessment centre and the tests you will undergo. Fear not – this topic will be covered in great depth in another chapter and you will also find a series of preparation tests at the end of this guide. For now, we will help you to consider whether or not you are the right personal fit for a train company.

UNDERSTANDING YOUR CHANCES

Remember, there are thousands of applicants vying for the same position as you. Therefore, unless you have a sterling application and/or CV, your chances are relatively low. It is crucial that you make every effort to present an excellent application, work hard to prepare for the tests and put in the effort during your pre-interview preparation. Go all out to be in the top 1% of applicants-it is achievable!

THE ORDER OF THE SELECTION PROCESS

How does the application process work with London Underground? This is an important thing to understand for potential applicants. Below, you will find a brief outline covering the entire process from beginning to end.

First, you will fill out and turn in your application. You might complete a physical application, or you might complete a virtual application – both are available from TfL. As mentioned, ensure that the application is filled out completely, accurately and legibly. Turn it in as soon as you have completed it, as waiting even a few days will reduce your chances of being accepted for the next stage.

Once your application has been submitted, you will have to wait for a decision. This can be a lengthy period, but have patience. Eventually you will receive a response to your application, which will invite you to complete a 30 minute, multiple choice ability test. You will either be asked to complete the questions online, or in person. The test will examine your ability to perform skills such as numerical calculation, or understand written information. You will be given several sample questions prior to the test, so that you can familiarise yourself with the process. On the SHL website, you can complete practice tests and questions to get yourself ready for the process. When taking the real test, make sure you find a quiet location where you won't be disturbed. This is a vitally important part of the process, and requires 100% of your concentration. This is also good practice for similar tests that you will be required to take later in the application process. If you are successful, you will receive an invitation to attend an assessment centre, informing you of when and where you should appear for further testing.

At the assessment centre, you will undergo rigorous testing. This will take the form of both individual, and group examination, in several key areas. This will include: psychometric testing, aptitude testing and personality testing. These are designed to give the company information about your skills, aptitude and attitude, and much more. The information gathered during these tests, as well as whether you pass or fail, will determine whether or not you are offered a place on the training course. You will also be required to take a competency based, face to face interview with assessors, who will further determine whether you are suitable for the role. Sometimes, the assessment centre will be split in two sessions, morning and afternoon. The weaker candidates will be 'cut' after the opening sessions, and the stronger candidates will progress to the later stages. This will depend solely upon the assessment centre which you are attending. When you receive your confirmation email, contact TFL or the centre itself for more details.

Assuming that you pass the assessment centre, you will wait for a few more days until you are notified about where to report for training. This will mark the beginning of a long period of intensive training. You will undergo some rigorous theory work, as well as hands-on training with different types of trains and their associated systems.

Finally, after several weeks of study, you should emerge as a fully qualified train driver for the London Underground. Once you have been given your first assignment, you can truly begin your career as a London Underground Train Driver. The rest, as they say, is history.

So, you have received a positive response to your application and have been invited to attend the assessment centre. This can be both exciting and daunting. What will the assessment centre be like? What sorts of tests will you have to undergo? What should you expect? This chapter will walk you through the assessment centre experience, and remove some of the mystery from the process.

WHAT IS THE ASSESSMENT CENTRE?

At the assessment centre, you will undergo a series of tests, and a face to face interview. These are designed to determine your strengths and weaknesses, your abilities and aptitudes. This is usually the third part of the selection process, if you do not pass these tests, you will not be invited to the training centre.

There are several different tests that will be administered, and you will likely be part of a group of other applicants. However, it is also possible that you will be alone. If you are the only one being tested, you can expect the process to take less time than if you are part of a group. The reason for this is that, in a group, you must move on at the pace of the slowest member, whereas doing it on your own allows you to move at your own pace.

In a group setting, you should expect your assessment tests to last about 3.5 to 4 hours total. If you are taking them on your own, then you will most likely finish before this point – 2 hours is average for this. All of the tests administered are time-sensitive, but you will be provided with practice tests prior to attempting the real thing, and there are no time limits on these.

What tests will you undertake? What is the purpose of each test? Below, you will find a list of the possible tests you might encounter in an assessment centre, as well as what your results will tell the test administrator about you.

THE GROUP TEST

The group exercise requires you to work as part of a team, to come up with solutions to problems. You will be given various pieces of information about a proposal or plan, and then have 40 minutes to discuss the plan with your team members, and work out the advantages and disadvantages of the plan. You will be assessed on your ability to work as part of a team, your strength of personality (without being too pushy) and the competency of your responses.

Following the group exercise you will be given 30 minutes to produce a written report on the conclusions of your group discussion. This will assess your ability to communicate in writing, present information in a clear and structured manner and remember key details.

THE ENGLISH TEST

This test is given for several different reasons. For one thing, it tests your basic reading comprehension, your vocabulary and your reading speed. It also tests your proficiency in the English language.

However, the true purpose of this test is to make sure that you are capable of ingesting information and then relaying that information without errors. This should present no problems so long as you are proficient in English and have a good memory for the information being relayed.

TEST PREPARATION TIPS

Preparing for the English portion of the assessment centre should not be a problem. After all, you have to be proficient with reading, writing and understanding the English language to hold this position. If you struggle with reading, now is the time to brush up on your skills.

THE PA TEST

Another test you will undergo is the use of the public address system (PA). You will actually go through three different stages during this test. First, you will receive information. Second, you will write down the announcement to be made over the PA system. Finally, you will record your announcement for review later by the review panel.

This test is designed to provide answers to several different questions. First, you will be graded on the accuracy of your written announcement compared to the original information. Second, you will be graded on the quality of your written announcement. Finally, you will be graded on the quality of your verbal announcement.

TEST PREPARATION TIPS

Preparing for the PA system test can be done quite easily. Simply pick a verbal announcement from a TV or radio source and write down the information. You can then reformulate that information into an announcement in your own words. Make sure that the wording is direct, understandable and actionable. Now, simply practice speaking that announcement aloud. You might even choose to record yourself speaking and play it back later.

MECHANICAL COMPREHENSION TEST

Obviously, as a train driver, you will have to work closely with machinery of different sorts all the time. While you might not always be the one responsible for making changes or repairs, it is essential that you know how different pieces of machinery work together. This test will show you diagrams of various mechanical elements, like wheels, gears and levers.

Your job will be to determine what the piece is, and how

it works with other pieces of machinery. What is the result of one piece working on another? Since you should have familiarity with different pieces of machinery to become a train operator, this should not be difficult.

This test is designed to ensure that you have a good working knowledge of mechanical design, and can correctly anticipate the result of an action or series of actions within a mechanical system.

TEST PREPARATION TIPS

If you intend to be a train driver, then you should have at least some basic knowledge of mechanical systems and how they work together. To prepare for this portion of the test, you can study simple groupings of gears and cogs, belts and pulleys and determine how each works and how each item in the grouping affects others. Car engines, block and tackle setups, and even some scientific children's toys can be used here to great extent.

You will find a sample test for this portion of the assessment towards the end of this guide.

FAULT FINDING TEST

This exercise is one of the more difficult that you will have to undergo. In essence, you need to study a series of actions, each of which depends on the others. You need to identify problems in the series of actions based on good or bad results. Tracing back through the action/decision timeline can be difficult, but determining which actions or decisions should have been different, in order to change the cumulative outcome, is also challenging.

The best advice for this section is to simply take a deep breath and concentrate on the problem at hand. If you panic, then this section will certainly be more difficult than if you were to calmly assess the test at hand and form reasoned decisions.

TEST PREPARATION TIPS

Finding the faults in a series of actions or decisions can be tough. Logic is your best friend here. You must simply start from one point and work your way toward the other, identifying the results of each action and how they might have differed if another action had been taken, or if the primary action had been modified. Often, this is easiest to do in reverse, taking known results and comparing them to the causation (action that caused the result).

You will find a sample test for this portion of the assessment towards the end of this guide.

COMPUTER TESTING

You will likely encounter two different computer tests. These are not designed to test your knowledge of computer systems. Rather, they relate directly to the job you will be doing as a train driver.

The first test involves watching a computer screen for a specified period of time and selecting particular groups of objects shown on it. This test is designed to test your concentration, and should be relatively easy to pass so long as you are able to pay attention to what you are doing.

The second test will involve a simulated array, and will use a computer in conjunction with pedals and a special keyboard. The test is designed to assess your reaction times, and your accuracy (both in actions and in decision making). You will respond to lights, symbols and sounds via the keyboard and the pedals. If you have ever spent any time playing video games, then this should not be difficult at all.

TEST PREPARATION TIPS

Preparing for these two types of computer tests is not terribly difficult. Of course, it helps if you are familiar with computers and simulators (video games). To help boost your memory and concentration, you can use flashcards or any number of memory type games. To boost your hand-eye coordination and reaction times, you can play simulator games, or even practice sports in which you have to have good hand-eye coordination and fast responses.

You will find a sample test for this portion of the assessment towards the end of this guide.

THE MEDICAL EXAMINATION AND TESTING

Once you have completed all the assessment tests, it will be time to go for your physical evaluation. You will be thoroughly checked by a medical practitioner.

What will they be looking for in the physical examination? This is a standard physical, and they will be checking your basic health and fitness levels. You should expect a full examination, including flexibility testing, lung capacity testing and more. However, this is not a strenuous test, so you should have no worries on that score.

After your physical, you will be given a full eye examination. As has been mentioned previously, good eyesight is an important requirement for train drivers. However, this does not mean that you will be excluded if you require corrective lenses, such as eyeglasses or contact lenses. This test is simply designed to determine the quality of your eyesight and whether or not you need corrective lenses. You will also be asked if you have had laser eye surgery, as this is an important consideration for hiring train drivers.

Finally, you will be required to pass a drug test for employment. This test will check for common recreational drugs, prescription drugs and even alcohol that is in your system. If you drink, it is wise to avoid doing so for at least a day prior to the testing to ensure a clean test result.

If you regularly take a prescription medication to manage a health condition, then you need to make the testers and the company aware of this prior to the test, so that those results can be ruled out. You might be required to provide the physician's prescription as proof that you actually require the medication. This is a common requirement and should pose no problem to you.

AFTER THE ASSESSMENT

Following the testing process, you will be interviewed face to face by an assessor, or group of assessors. This is an extremely important part of the process. In the next chapter, we will give you detailed information on the interview, the type of questions you should expect and the best way to answer them.

CHAPTER 5

HOW TO PASS THE LONDON UNDERGROUND TRAIN DRIVERS INTERVIEW

After performing the group exercises and ability tests, you will be invited into a room to interview face to face with an assessor. This will make or break your chances of going onto the following stage, so therefore it is important to be prepared. In this chapter you will learn more about how the interview will proceed, as well as how you can prepare for it.

UNDERSTANDING THE INTERVIEW

The chances are you will not be ushered into the interview room immediately after completing your tests. Rather, you will likely have to wait for a short period of time. This gives you a chance to mentally run down a list of questions and answers, ensuring that you are prepared for what is to come. When you actually get into the interview, you will find that you are faced with two different people. There will normally be a member of Human Resources, and a manager present. Be prepared to answer questions from both.

What sort of questions might you have to answer here? Understanding and being prepared for these questions is very important. Below, you will find an entire section dedicated to this topic.

POTENTIAL QUESTIONS DURING THE INTERVIEW

Here are some examples of questions that you will be asked, as well as why these questions are important. Often, understanding the underlying reason for the question will help you answer more completely. Make certain that you answer each question honestly and accurately – many of your answers will be checked against your records after the interview.

Understanding and preparing for these questions is very important. Below you will find an entire section dedicated to this topic.

Do you have any previous experience doing shift work?
As has been mentioned, train driving is shift based work.
You will usually be on a rotating shift. Previous experience
with shift work is a good thing, but it is not necessary. You
simply need to make sure that the interviewer knows that
you are willing to do the work and that you understand what
it entails.

**Give an example of an emergency situation in which you
have been involved. How did you react to the situation?**
The interviewer is looking for an example of an emergency
that you have encountered either personally or professionally.
This might be an auto accident, an unexpected situation
involving a wounded person or something entirely different.
What the interviewer wants to know is how you reacted to
that situation – what actions you took, how you handled
yourself and what decisions you made. This is an important
question, as train drivers must be prepared to handle
emergencies whilst working solo shifts.

Why do you want to be a train driver?
This seems like a generic question. However, it is not. Your
reasons for wanting to be a train driver are very important, as
they speak to just how long you will remain in the position.
You might have wanted to drive a train since your childhood,
or you might like the challenge of providing service to people
from all over the world. Regardless, your answer will tell the
interviewer whether or not you will be a long-term employee.

How would a work colleague describe you?
Why does this particular question matter? This is designed
to give the interviewer insight into how you handle yourself
on the job, how you interact with other people and how you
might be expected to perform on the job as a driver. It also
shows your level of honesty.

Give an example of a time when you had to work as a member of a team. How did the experience turn out? What did you learn?

Team work is an important part of being a train driver. Even though you will be operating the train alone, you will still be an important member of a team. Your team will consist of engineers, controllers and other officers. You must be able to cite how well you work in a team environment and more.

What do you know about the company?

This is an important question. The interviewer wants to see how much you know about London Underground, and TfL. If you are at all interested in being a train driver, then you should have a good knowledge base of the company, its policies, procedures and more. In short, the more you know about the company, the better. Of course, the interviewer does not expect you to have encyclopaedic knowledge here.

How often are you out of work due to sickness?

This is an essential question. Your answer here must be honest, because they will check your record from previous employment periods. Make sure that you give an accurate account of any absences due to sickness and explain any long periods of ill health or frequent absences. This is also important because it gives the interviewer information about how reliable you will be in the position and how often you might miss work as a driver.

Have you had corrective vision surgery (laser/Lasik eye surgery)?

Good vision is an important trait for a train driver to possess. You will rely on your vision while driving, to navigate the routes and to detect and avoid obstacles and hazards in your path. Corrective eye surgery is not necessarily a mark against you, but it is information that your interviewer will need to know.

How will you arrive at the job for an early morning shift (3 AM)?

Here, the interviewer is looking for assurance that you will be able to make it to work for your early shifts. Someone who is relying on public transport to get to work is unlikely to make a reliable train driver. This is because you will not have access to this transport at 3 AM. The interviewer wants to know that you have your own transportation and that you will be able to be reliable in arriving on time for your shifts.

Have you ever worked alone, or spent long periods on your own in a hobby?

This is an important question as well. As a train driver, the majority of your shift will be spent alone in the cab of the train. Not everyone is able to handle this type of situation well. What the interviewer is looking for is experience and assurance that you can handle time alone equably. Obviously, this is an important consideration for this type of job.

Have you ever had to study to pass a course/become certified before?

As you will have to undergo train driver training, the interviewer is looking for assurance that you know how to study. While it might seem a bit odd, not everyone has the skills to absorb knowledge in a classroom setting, or through independent study. Obviously, they want to hire those with the most aptitude and best chance of success.

How do you handle physical fatigue?

While driving a train is not horribly demanding in the physical sense, it can be quite fatiguing. The interviewer is looking for confirmation that you will be able to stay awake and alert after a long shift. Train drivers must be alert and capable of quick reactions at all times, regardless of their fatigue level.

How do you handle stress in your life/on the job?

Stress can be a big factor in driving trains. Delays, hazards, passengers, other co-workers and other factors can all add to your stress level. The interviewer wants to know that you can perform your job adequately despite these stressors, as those who cannot are not good candidates for this particular position.

How do you prevent yourself from losing concentration in a boring environment?

This can be a bit misleading. While driving a train can be somewhat tedious, there will be ample excitement at times. What the interviewer really wants to know is how you maintain your concentration and focus for long periods of time. How do you ensure that you are awake and aware at the tail end of a route or shift?

How well do you handle repetitive tasks?
Give an example.

Repetitive tasks can become routine, boring and tiresome. While you will certainly have to deal with many different things during the course of an average shift, you will find that the actual driving portion is very repetitive. How do you handle this type of situation?

Name a few stations that the company serves.

Here, the interviewer is looking for more information about your knowledge of the company and the areas in which it operates. Familiarity is a good thing here; there is no need for in-depth knowledge about company history, but familiarity with routes covered and stations served will be a good thing.

In addition to the questions listed above, you will also be asked other questions based on your answers. The best option is to answer all questions as honestly, directly and accurately as possible. If an interviewer feels that they need more information about something, he or she will ask you. You will also have to face long periods during which the interviewer writes notes about your answers. This can be unnerving for some people. Be patient and calm – so long as you are able to be honest in your answers, your interview should be fine.

In addition, you will probably find that the interviewers question you about the various lines and depots. The point here is to find out which ones are closest to you, which are the most appealing to your situation and which ones interest you the most. There is no guarantee that you will be placed on a line or in a depot of your choosing, but they do take your location into account. If you are willing to relocate for work, you need to say so during this portion, as well.

AFTER THE INTERVIEW

After the completion of your interview, you should have a feeling that things went well. However, it can be easy for doubt to creep in there. This is natural, and is not a true indicator of how your interview went. Almost everyone who undergoes such an interview will eventually doubt their success during the process. Be patient and wait for a response from the company.

It can take quite some time for you to receive a response to your interview – several days at the very least. You might receive notification in the mail, or you might receive a phone call. Regardless, when you receive your notification, you will also be informed of your training class, where it is located and how long it will last.

As a note, London Underground has increased their training scheme from nine weeks to 22 weeks. This is because many direct recruits who did not have any previous experience with the Underground were finding the nine-week scheme too intensive and the company was not able to bring in the number of quality drivers required. Therefore, be prepared to spend 22 weeks in basic driver training. After that, you will be assigned a route and a depot, and will receive an additional four weeks of training based on route/depot specific needs.

CHAPTER 6

UNDERGOING TRAINING TO BECOME A LONDON UNDERGROUND TRAIN DRIVER

Training is an essential ingredient of your career. After passing the interview, you will officially be a driver trainee. You will earn a base salary during this period, as well. However, this salary is only a fraction of what you will earn as a full train driver. Of course, to earn that title, you will need to complete your training. This is a very important period during your career, and not everyone who enters training will complete it. This chapter will give you an overview of what to expect during this time.

THE POTENTIAL FOR FAILURE

While this is certainly not a pretty topic, it is one that has to be broached early on in this chapter. The simple fact of the matter is that not all trainees will go on to become train drivers. There can be a considerable amount of pressure during these training courses, and you must be able to fully ingest safety rules and regulations, operating procedures, emergency procedures and much more.

Obviously, given the immense responsibility that comes with driving a train, the company cannot afford to let trainees go on to become drivers if they do not have the knowledge and skills required, or if they are unable to handle the pressure such a position brings with it. So long as you study hard and are able to retain the information taught, you will do fine.

AN OVERVIEW OF THE TRAINING PROCESS

You will find that there are several distinct sections to your training. Each of these will conclude with an assessment test given by a licensed instructor. You will also spend a considerable amount of time in cab simulators and within the cab of an operating train.

The first few days will be an introductory period. You will

get to know the other trainees within your class, and begin learning more about the London Underground. In fact, the first stage can be considered London Underground 101. You will learn about train composition, the history of London Underground, signal types, track layout and more. You will also visit the London Underground Museum to get more in-depth knowledge about the evolution of the system.

The second portion of your training will be operational proce-dures training, or OPT. This is the "rules and regulations" pe-riod, during which you will learn the various rules that govern the operation of underground trains and the Underground in general. Each module here must be passed in order to move on. If the instructor does not feel that you have made sufficient progress, you will have to review the material again and retake the test once more. However, not passing is not an immediate "out", so you have a bit of relief from this.

The next segment of your training will be Supply and Distribution of Traction Current – learning how to turn on and off the electricity to the train, more about rail gaps and how emergency switching setups work. These are very important, and the study here can be quite intensive. You will learn the basics of electricity, as well as how these are applied to the London Underground system.

Next up, you will begin studying Signalling Systems. This course will take several days, or even a full week, as you must learn how to identify all the various signals by heart, as well as how the signals operate. You will learn about semiautomatic signals, automatic signals, trainstops, junction indications, signalling overlaps, shunt signalling, mechanical interlocking, electrical interlocking and numerous other subjects here.

Track safety is another important element of your training. You will study safety on the track and in the depot, as well as learning more about traffic hours and how safety applies here. Eventually, you will take a "Track Walk", during which you will need to show what you have learned during the course thus far. A computer-based test is given after this, and you must pass if you are to continue. Failure of this examination will result in your expulsion from the course.

The test is simple enough, and is composed of multiple-choice questions. You simply select the right answer to the question posed. However, this does require that you have learned the material thus far. A passing score is 80% correct, and will result in you being Track Certified. You will also find that the test is timed; after the time is up, you cannot continue answering questions.

Next up, you will begin more intensive training. You will learn more about passing signals at danger (SPADS), how to use your radio properly, more about station overruns, moving in the wrong direction, how to protect staff in the tunnels, how to use mirrors and monitors, and more. One frightening, though highly important, topic covered now is what to do in the case of a person under the train. These might be accident victims, or they might be suicides. However, this can be a horrific reality and you need to understand how to deal with it.

You will also discover that a much greater emphasis is placed on teamwork during this time. You will find yourself working closely with your classmates, and if you are not able to work well in a team environment, this will become readily apparent. If you are unable to work well with another individual on your team, you need to mention this to your instructor, as teams will need to be rearranged to prevent personality clashes and a negative impact to your class as a whole.

The final assessment for this portion is a test of some 50 questions. However, each of these questions will have subsequent questions that must be answered. Most of these are questions about actions to take in a sequence of events, "If A happens, do you do B, C, or D? If B happens as a result of A, do you choose to A, C or E?" However, if you miss an answer, you immediately lose the question and a considerable portion of your overall score.

If you fail the test by a certain amount, you will be given a second attempt to take it. However, if you score below 50% on the test, you will be automatically ejected from the program. You are eligible to re-enter the program at a later date, but you will be removed from your current class and have to start from the beginning, with the application process.

Next, you will visit a working depot and explore the various signals and equipment found here. You will also take a closer look at how roster sheets and duty sheets play a role in your daily responsibilities. Finally, you will study Roles and Responsibilities. While the subject sounds rather daunting, it simply shows you how you, as a train operator, fit into the daily running of London Underground, and your responsibilities therein.

Finally, you will delve into the topic of trains and how they work. This section is very comprehensive and in-depth, and it contains some of the most important information that you will receive in your training. Everything you learn during this period will have an affect on your job after graduating, so it is essential that you are able to ingest and retain it all.

The formal title for this section is Principals of Train Equipment, or POTE. You will find that it involves a great deal of classroom work, as well as visiting an operating train and viewing the various components and systems firsthand. You will learn how a train is made up, how the different on-board systems interact with each other and the details of the various equipment found on trains. You will also learn more about how compressed air works in a train, how the traction current is taken in and used by the components on the train and the role of batteries, fuses and circuits in the train. Of course, you will also cover the braking system and how the doors operate.

This is a very mechanical-intensive section. If you have little aptitude for mechanical processes, you will be struggling very hard to keep up at this point. The course is designed this way on purpose. The intention is to weed out any recruits who do not have the aptitude to handle operating a train and all the various systems that are used to operate it. While you might not ever need to know how the braking system works, that knowledge can be vital in the case of an emergency.

You will also be exposed to new terminology during this portion of your education. Some very technical terms will be introduced to you. The best advice is to add them to your vocabulary immediately – learn their meanings and become familiar with how those terms are used. This will help you decipher the various diagrams and schematics of the train systems and components that you will have to study.

When your theory lessons have been completed, you will then put them to use on a real train. This is an essential portion of your training. Theoretical knowledge is all well and good, but real, hands-on experience is the best way to become familiar with the systems you will be working so closely with in the future. You will visit a depot and will then begin learning the ropes. This will include: opening up a train, the process of charging the air-lines and learning how to use the equipment in the cab. You will also learn how to open doors when there is no compressed available, what various line bursts sound like and the impact these bursts can have on a train. You might even be given the opportunity to try some of these systems and equipment out on your own to make you more familiar with them and their operation.

At the end of this, there is a written assessment course. Once again, you will need to score the same percentages to carry on. If you do not have the grades to pass on the first try, you will be given a second attempt. However, as with the previous exam, a second failure or an initial grade of 50% or lower will result in expulsion from the course.

At this point, you will find that your class is split into two segments. One segment will be for those destined for the deep trains, and the other group will be made up of those destined for subsurface trains. There is a considerable difference between these two trains, even though they use the same basic equipment and their functions are almost identical.

A NOTE ON TRAIN TYPES

Deep trains, or Deep Tube trains, are smaller and more compact than their subsurface brethren are. This is because the tubes are smaller in diameter than the subsurface cuts. On Deep Tube trains, more equipment must be mounted inside the train, so some equipment is located in different places (fuses are located under seats, for example, where they are mounted externally on subsurface trains).

TRAINING CONTINUES

You will now begin learning more about the type of trains that you will be operating. Essentially, this is only an expansion on what you have already learned, but you will be studying these topics in much greater detail. You will also be introduced to troubleshooting the operation of your train. In essence, this boils down to finding the fault in the system that is preventing the train from operating. There is a handy acronym for this process: PLATO. Following this process should help you identify the problem area, and correct it, getting the train moving once more. What is PLATO? In essence, it can be boiled down to the following:

PL: Pilot Light – The pilot light is an indicator that shows the doors are closed. If the doors are not closed, then the train will not move. The doors must be closed before you can make any progress, and these are often the primary cause of a malfunction. Blow fuses, a person blocking the door and keeping it from closing and other problems can all be responsible for no pilot light.

A: Air – Compressed air is an essential ingredient of a properly operating train. As much of the equipment aboard your train is pneumatic, a lack of sufficient air pressure can certainly prevent the train from operating. The best indicator of this condition is the pressure gauge located in the train's cab. Burst lines, compressor failure and other causes can create a drop in air pressure sufficient to leave a train motionless.

T: Traction Current – Without traction current, your train has no power. If the train has stopped over a rail gap, or if there is a lack of power for some other reason, then your train will be immobile. Check for the motor alternator light first; if it is off, then you have lost traction current.

O: Overloads – If your overload switches have dropped out, then the train will be immobile. You can reengage these with the Overload Set button in the cab of the train.

This should (in theory) get the train moving again, if this is the cause of the problem.

PLATO is not the only check that you will need to learn, but it is the foundation for most of the rest of them. Depending on the result of these checks, you will then take other actions, as you will learn during this period in your training.

After exhaustive training in finding faults, learning how the equipment works and mastering the handling of your train, it will be time for your final evaluation. This is given in a one-on-one situation, and can last as long as 3.5 hours. You will be given a time to appear for your examination; make sure that you are on time, or you will affect the schedule for those classmates following you in the rotation. The final examinations for your class will be split up over the course of several days, in order to ensure that everyone has ample time for the test.

This test will be a mixture of written exam and a hands-on demonstration of operating a train and finding faults in the system. You will open up the train and your instructor will set the faults that you are to find. You will be required to describe the steps you are taking to find the faults and why those particular steps are required.

The next step, assuming that you pass this portion of the training, will be Driver Training. You will also find that you are moved up to full train operator status, and will begin earning the same pay as other operators and enjoying the other benefits of this position.

Driver training is a critical course, and forms the core of the knowledge and skills that you will use on a daily basis in your job. For this portion, you will usually be assigned to the line on which you will operate on a regular basis, unless there are mitigating circumstances. You will follow the direction of an Instructor Operator – an operator who you will study under – for the duration of this training. In addition, you will be operating live trains, in actual service at this point. The only real difference between this and your final position will be the presence (and instruction) of your I/O.

Your instructor will see to your training as he or she sees fit, but you will have to prep and inspect the train, take it out into service, speak with the control centre, learn how to communicate with the Line Controller and much more during this time. This period is set to give you a firm foundation of real world experience on which to draw during your time as an actual driver.

The final test for this portion of your training will be a mixture of written and multiple choice. You will also find that it draws from all areas of your training, not just from the driver training portion of your experience. While it is somewhat easier than other tests you have taken thus far, it is far more than a mere formality.

After passing this test, you will move on to learning how other stock operates, and then on to your road testing. The reason that you need to learn how to operate different stock is obvious – you need to be familiar with as many models as possible so that you can drive them if need be. This period will involve actual study of the equipment on the stock, as well as a period of observation riding with another driver as they conduct their normal routes. When this is done, you will embark on your road training portion, which is another very important part.

Road training is an incredibly important part of your education. You will find that this involves far more than simply learning how to handle a train to a greater degree. The entire point of this portion is to help you learn the various routes, intersections, reverse points, and other parts of the line. This portion of your training will end with a road test with your duty manager. Your duty manager will either certify you as competent or not – there is really no reason why you should not be rated as competent, though, if you have made it this far in your training. After the road testing portion, you will be ready for your first day as a solo train driver.

CHAPTER 7

FREQUENTLY ASKED QUESTIONS (FAQ)

There are many different questions that you might have about becoming a train driver for the London Underground. This chapter is dedicated to providing answers to the most common of these questions, in as much detail as possible.

THE QUESTIONS AND ANSWERS

Q: What do I have to do to start the application process with London Underground?

A: You must submit an application with the TfL through their website, or through the mail. The website is: http://www.TfL. gov.uk

Q: How old do you have to be to become a London Underground train driver?

A: You must be at least 18 years old to become a driver trainee. Generally, the company prefers you to be at least 21 years old to be a full train driver.

Q: Is there a graduate scheme available?

A: Yes, the TfL has both graduate and other schemes.

Q: Will my foreign train driver certification work to get on with London Underground?

A: No, you will have to go through the same process as all other candidates, though your training will certainly weigh in your favour.

Q: Can existing train drivers circumvent the regular hiring process?

A: To a certain extent. You will still need to submit your application and your other credentials, as well as proof of your safety record and other criteria.

Q: What happens after I submit my application with TfL?

A: You will receive a response via phone or mail instructing you where to go for your interview.

Q: Will the interview be conducted by phone or in person?

A: TfL uses both phone and in-person interviews. You will be informed of what to expect.

Q: How long will the interview take to complete?

A: Generally, you should allot several hours for completion of the interview.

Q: Is my London Underground certification able to be transferred to other train companies?

A: Sometimes, but not in all cases. You will have to ensure that you meet the company's requirements. In some cases, other railway companies require additional training because they run aboveground trains.

Q: How will I know if I have passed my interview?

A: You will be mailed an invitation or notified by phone of where to go to start your training.

Q: How long will training last?

A: Training is currently set for 22 weeks. This does change from time to time, as new programmes and schedules are introduced.

OTHER OPTIONS

Whilst being a train driver for London Underground can be enormously rewarding, you might find that you want to branch out a bit. There are numerous other railway companies operating around London and throughout the rest of the UK. You can turn this to your advantage, and find employment with another company if you desire.

One difference that you will find is that most railway companies require a longer training period than London Underground. This is because other companies operate in different environments. The Underground has its own peculiarities as far as environmental concerns, but other railway companies must deal with many other issues.

For instance, you will have to learn how to handle adverse weather, such as ice, sleet, snow and hail. You will also find that not all of these trains carry passengers – hauling freight is a different matter from managing a commuter train. Finally, you will find that these companies have very different trains. Diesel locomotives take the place of electric trains. This, alone, can be a very different change, as the technology is not similar in any respect.

What does this mean for you? Simply put, it means that your certification probably will not transfer over, unless you are seeking employment with another subway line. In this instance, you can almost be certain that your certification will carry over, though you might have to take an assessment test to ensure that you meet that company's requirements.

However, you should find that the testing and training portion is much simpler if you have already passed the requirements for London Underground. While you will have to learn the differences between aboveground and underground trains, you will at least have a firm basis on which to build that knowledge.

CONCLUSION

Becoming a London Underground train driver can be an excellent option for many different people. If you have a love of trains, or if you simply want a personally and financially rewarding career route, this could be the perfect job for you.

Following the steps outlined throughout this book will ensure that you are able to understand every part of the hiring and training process, as well as help make certain that you are able to get the job that you want. As a London Underground train driver, you stand to earn a decent living, you will have many different advancement opportunities, and you will be able to help others at the same time.

All the information that you need to get your career started can be found in the preceding pages – good luck and enjoy your new career!

CHAPTER 8

SAMPLE TEST
QUESTIONS

DISCLAIMER

The tests that we have provided you within this section of the guide are for preparation purposes only. We do not claim that the tests are the same/similar to ones that you will be required to undertake during the London Underground Train Driver selection process. How2become Ltd are not responsible for anyone failing any part of the selection process as a result of the information/tests that are contained within this guide.

MECHANICAL COMPREHENSION TEST

During the Trainee Train Driver selection process you will be required to sit a mechanical comprehension test that consists of 36 questions. You will have just 18 minutes in which to complete the test. Mechanical comprehension tests are an assessment that measures an individual's aptitude to learn mechanical skills. The tests are usually multiple-choice in nature and present simple, frequently encountered mechanisms and situations. The majority of mechanical comprehension tests require a working knowledge of basic mechanical operations and the application of physical laws. On the following pages I have provided you with a number of example questions to help you prepare for the tests. Work through them as quickly as possible but remember to go back and check which ones you get wrong; more importantly, make sure you understand *how* the correct answer is reached.

In this particular exercise there are 20 questions and you have 10 minutes in which to answer them.

MECHANICAL COMPREHENSION TEST 1

Question 1

If Circle 'B' turns in a Clockwise direction, which way will circle 'A' turn?

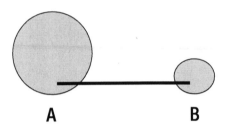

A. Clockwise

B. Anti-Clockwise

C. Backwards and forwards

D. It won't move

Answer [   ]

Question 2

Which square is carrying the heaviest load?

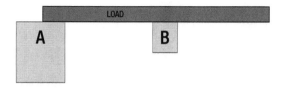

A. Square A

B. Square B

Answer [   ]

Question 3

Which pendulum will swing at the slowest speed?

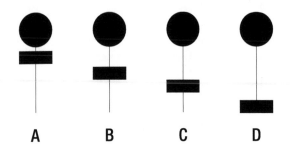

A   B   C   D

Answer

Question 4

If Cog 'A' turns in an anti-clockwise direction which way will Cog 'B' turn?

A. Clockwise

B. Anti-Clockwise

Answer

Question 5

If Cog 'B' moves in a clockwise direction, which way will Cog 'A' turn?

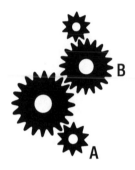

A. Clockwise

B. Anti-Clockwise

Answer

Question 6

Which shelf can carry the greatest load?

A. Shelf A

B. Shelf B

Answer [ ]

Question 7

At which point will the pendulum be travelling at the greatest speed?

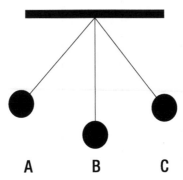

A   B   C

A. Point A

B. Point B

C. Point C

Answer [   ]

Question 8

At which point will the beam balance?

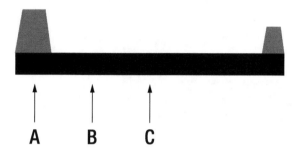

A. Point A

B. Point B

C. Point C

Answer

Question 9

If water is poured into the narrow tube, up to point 'X', what height would it reach in the wide tube?

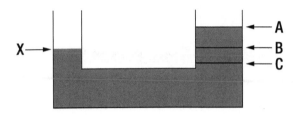

A. Point A

B. Point B

C. Point C

Answer [   ]

Question 10

At which point would Ball 'Y' have to be placed to balance out Ball 'X'?

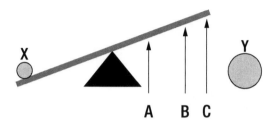

A. Point A

B. Point B

C. Point C

Answer

Question 11

If Cog 'A' turns anti-clockwise, which way will Cog 'F' turn?

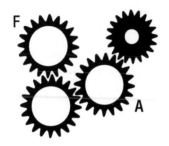

A. Cannot say

B. Clockwise

C. Anti-Clockwise

Answer [   ]

Question 12

Which post is carrying the heaviest load?

A. Both the Same

B. Post X

C. Post Y

Answer

Question 13

If water is poured in at Point D, which tube will overflow first?

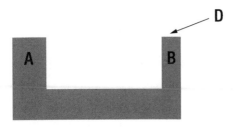

A. Tube A

B. Both the same

C. Tube B

Answer [   ]

Question 14

At which point would it be easier to haul up load X?

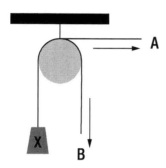

A. Both the Same

B. Point A

C. Point B

Answer

Question 15

If rope 'A' is pulled in the direction of the arrow, which way will wheel 'C' turn?

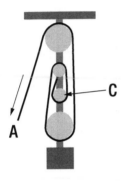

A. Clockwise

B. Anti-clockwise

C. It will not turn

Answer

Question 16

Which load is the heaviest?

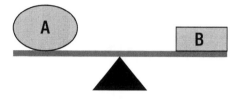

A. Load A

B. Load B

C. Both the same

Answer [   ]

Question 17

If rope 'A' is pulled in the direction of the arrow, which direction will Load 'Q' travel in?

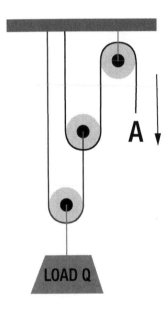

A. It will not move

B. Down

C. Up

Answer

Question 18

If circle 'X' turns anti-clockwise, which way will circle 'Y' turn?

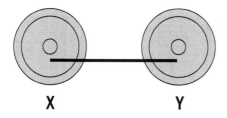

X   Y

 A. Anti-clockwise

 B. Clockwise

 C. Backwards and forwards

Answer [   ]

Question 19

Which pulley system will be the easiest to lift the bucket of water?

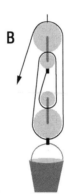

A. Both the Same

B. Pulley A

C. Pulley B

Answer [   ]

Question 20

At which point(s) will the pendulum be swinging the fastest?

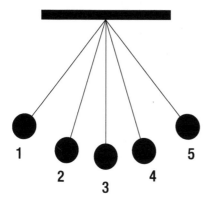

A. Point 1

B. Points 1 and 5

C. Points 3 and 5

D. Point 3

Answer

Now that you have completed mechanical comprehension exercise 1, check your answers carefully before moving onto the exercise 2.

ANSWERS TO MECHANICAL COMPREHENSION TEST 1

1. C

2. B

3. D

4. B

5. A

6. B

7. B

8. B

9. B

10. A

11. C

12. C

13. B

14. A

15. B

16. C

17. C

18. A

19. C

20. D

MECHANICAL COMPREHENSION TEST 2

During mechanical comprehension test 2 you have 10 minutes in which to answer the 20 questions.

Question 1

In the following cog and belt system, which cog will rotate the most number of times in an hour?

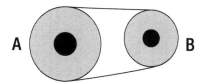

A. Cog A

B. Cog B

C. Both the same

Answer [   ]

Question 2

In the following cog and belt system, which cog will rotate the most number of times in thirty minutes?

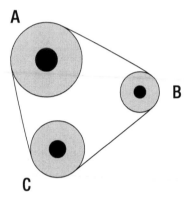

A. Cog A

B. Cog B

C. Both the same

Answer

Question 3

Which rope would be the easiest to pull the mast over with?

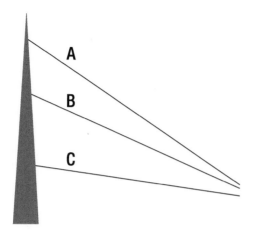

A. Rope A

B. Rope B

C. Rope C

Answer

Question 4

If cog A turns anti clockwise as indicated, which way will cog C turn?

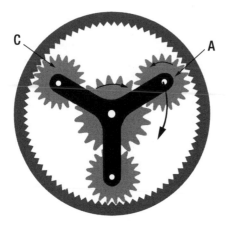

A. Clockwise

B. Anti-clockwise

C. Backwards and forwards

Answer

Question 5

If cog A turns clockwise, which way will cog D turn?

A. Clockwise

B. Anti-clockwise

C. Backwards and forwards

Answer [   ]

Question 6

If wheel D moves anticlockwise at a speed of 100 rpm, how will wheel B move and at what speed?

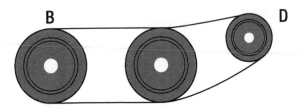

A. Clockwise faster

B. Clockwise slower

C. Anticlockwise faster

D. Anticlockwise slower

Answer [   ]

Question 7

Which is the best tool to use for tightening bolts?

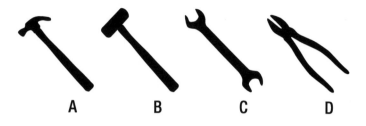

A   B   C   D

Answer [   ]

Question 8

In the following circuit, if switch A closes and switch B remains open, what will happen?

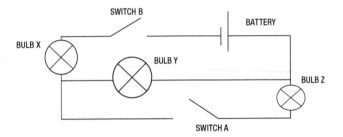

A. Bulbs X, Y, and Z will illuminate.

B. Bulb X will illuminate only.

C. Bulbs Y and Z will illuminate only.

D. No bulbs will illuminate.

Answer [   ]

Question 9

In the following circuit, if switch A closes, what will happen?

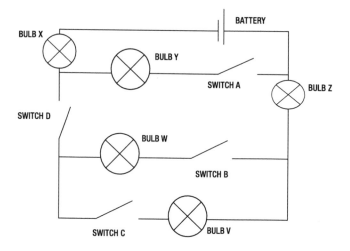

A. Bulbs V, W, X, Y, and Z will illuminate.

B. Bulb X and Y will illuminate only.

C. Bulbs X, Y and Z will illuminate only.

D. No bulbs will illuminate.

Answer [   ]

Question 10

The following four containers are filled with clean water to the same level, which is 2 metres in height. If you measured the pressure at the bottom of each container once filled with water, which container would register the highest reading? If you think the reading would be the same for each container then your answer should be E.

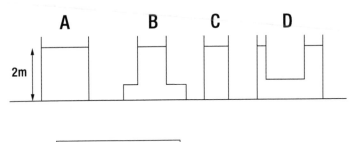

Answer [   ]

Question 11

Which of the following objects is the most unstable? If you think they are all the same, then choose F as your answer.

A   B   C   D   E

Answer [   ]

Question 12

How much weight will need to be placed at point X in order to balance out the beam?

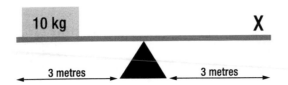

A. 10 kg

B. 15 kg

C. 20 kg

D. 30 kg

E. 100 kg

Answer

Question 13

Which post is carrying the greatest load?

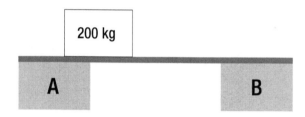

A. Post A

B. Post B

C. Both the same

Answer

Question 14

On the following weighing scales, which is the heaviest load?

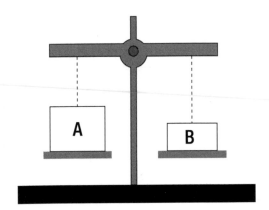

A. Load A

B. Load B

C. Both the same

Answer [   ]

Question 15

At which point should pressurised air enter the cylinder in order to force the piston downwards?

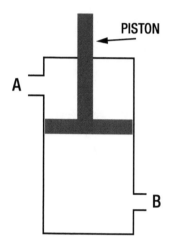

A. Point A

B. Point B

C. Both Point A and Point B

Answer

Question 16

At which point would you place the hook to keep the beam horizontal when lifted?

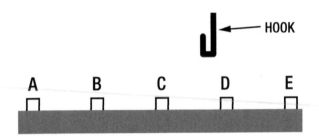

A. Point A

B. Point B

C. Point C

D. Point D

E. Point E

Answer ▢

Question 17

At which point will the ball be travelling the fastest?

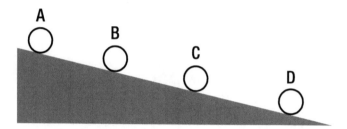

A. Point A

B. Point B

C. Point C

D. Point D

E. The same speed at each point

Answer [   ]

Question 18

If gear A moves to the right, which way will gear B move?

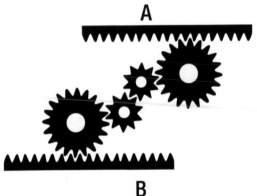

A. To the right

B. To the left

C. It won't move

D. Backwards and forward

Answer [　　　　　　　]

Question 19

At which point will the beam balance?

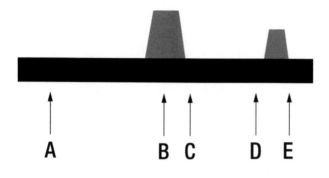

Answer [   ]

Question 20

Which is the heaviest load?

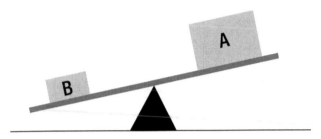

A. Load A

B. Load B

C. Both the same

Answer [   ]

Now that you have completed mechanical reasoning test 2, check your answers carefully before moving onto the next section of the guide.

ANSWERS TO MECHANICAL COMPREHENSION TEST 2

1. B

2. B

3. A

4. B

5. B

6. D

7. C

8. D

9. B

10. E

11. D

12. A

13. A

14. C

15. A

16. C

17. D

18. A

19. C

20. B

TIPS FOR PASSING THE MECHANICAL COMPREHENSION TEST

- During the actual test you will be assessed on speed <u>and</u> accuracy. Therefore, you are advised against random 'guessing'. In the build up to the test carry out lots of sample test questions.

- Work quickly through the test trying to get as many questions right as possible. If you come up against a difficult question, move on. But remember to leave a gap on the answer sheet!

- In the build up to the test study a car manual such as Haynes. This will give you an idea of how mechanical concepts work.

- Consider buying a GCSE Physics booklet such as 'Letts GCSE Revision Notes' (by Paul Levy – ISBN: 1840854758). I also strongly recommend the Mechanical Aptitude and Spatial Relation Test (Barron's Mechanical Aptitude & Spatial Relations Test) by Joel Wiesen. Both of these books are available for under £5 through Amazon.co.uk.

THE CHECKING TEST

The Checking Test is a two part exam, which requires you to listen to a tape or CD. You will also be given a printed page of information, which will be taken away from you when the audio recording has finished. After it has finished, you will have seven minutes to answer 18 multiple choice questions based on the information you have just heard and read about.

On the following page I have provided you with a sample passage that you must read for four minutes only. You are permitted to take notes during the four minute period. Once the four minutes are up turn the page and answer the questions without referring to your notes or the passage.

TEST 1

You have 4 minutes only to read the following passage and take notes before answering the questions supplied by the tutor.

Train tracks are made up of three main components: the metal rails, the sleepers that sit firmly underneath the rails and the ballast – the crushed rock segments that form a bed for the tracks to lie in.

A tamping machine, or a ballast tamper, is a machine that can be used for raising, straightening and altering the tracks. It is a machine that compresses the track ballast (the crushed segments of rock) under the rail track in order to make it more durable. Originally, this work was done manually, whereby labourers would use beaters as a way of pressing down the rock. Despite being faster, more accurate, efficient and less intensive, tamping machines are essential for the production and usage of creating stable tracks from concentre, typically weighing 250 kg.

For train tracks to work efficiently, the alignment of the tracks must be seamless. The sleepers that sit firmly underneath the rails, must also sit firmly in the crushed rock. If a track has been used for many years, or changes to the track have been made, the alignment of all three components needs to be altered in order to remain stable and effective. The gaps in the underlying rock bed need to be filled so that the sleepers do not move as a train passes along. This allows the train to run smoothly and ultimately reduces noise, vibrations and more importantly, any hazards.

Tamping machines can be used to fix these gaps by placing them on the track. It then conducts vibrations with hydraulic 'fingers' to remove all the gaps in the ballast, and align the track up. These machines are very noisy and often cause disruption. Not only are the machines themselves noisy, but they also trigger track alarms which act as a warning sign for workers of approaching trains.

Most tamping jobs are conducted during the night, in order to avoid disrupting train services. By conducting this job at night, therefore can affect nearby neighbourhoods for one or two nights. Due to tamping machines being a part of regular maintenance work, Train Operating Companies are often unable to notify neighbourhoods that may be disturbed.

Question 1

Name **one** component that makes up the train tracks. Three **possible** answers.

Answer [   ]

Question 2

What is the name of the machine that is used in order to compress the crushed rock underneath the rail tracks?

A – Tampering machine

B – Tangent machine

C – Hydraulics machine

D – Tamping machine

E – Tramping machine

Answer [   ]

Question 3

What is the typical weight of the concrete used in the production process?

A – 150 kg

B – 200 kg

C – 250 kg

D – 300 kg

E – 350 kg

Answer [   ]

Question 4

The machine compresses the rock underneath the tracks, in order to make the tracks more....

    A – Flexible

    B – Diverse

    C – Tangent

    D – Resistant

    E – Durable

Answer

Question 5

Whereabouts are the sleepers positioned?

    A – Underneath the ballast

    B – To the side of the ballast

    C – Underneath the rails

    D – To the side of the rails

    E – On top of the rails

Answer

Question 6

What is the main job of the machine?

    A – To compress the rock

    B – To align the rails

    C – To generate vibrations

    D – To assist the trains mobility

    E – To fix any gaps and voids in the track alignment

Answer

Question 7

What does these machines often trigger?

A – Signals

B – Mobility

C – Light

D – Alarms

E – Cannot be determined

Answer ⬚

Question 8

The alarms have been triggered. What is the reason for the alarm?

A – The sound of the job completed

B – To warn workers of an approaching train

C – The sound of the job beginning

D – The warn neighbours of work in progress

E – Cannot be determined

Answer ⬚

Question 9

What time, day or night, are tamping machines often used?

Answer ⬚

Question 10

What does this machinery conduct? Two answers needed.

A – Heat

B – Vibrations

C – Light

D – Noise

E – Mobility

Answer

Question 11

How was this job done originally?

Answer

Question 12

How often are the neighbourhoods living close by, notified of work with these machines?

A – Very often

B – Often

C – Neutral

D – Hardly ever

E – Never

Answer

Question 13

What is another name of the type of machine used?

Answer [ ]

Question 14

Why might the train track have gaps in the ballast?

A – Animals digging holes underneath the train tracks

B – The rock has eroded

C – The tracks have been used for many years

D – The infrastructure was not made correctly

E – Cannot be determined

Answer [ ]

ANSWERS TO TEST 1, SECTION 1

Q1. Metal rails, the sleepers or the ballast – you are only asked for one answer, and so any of these answers will be correct.

Q2. D = tamping machine

Q3. C = 250 kg

Q4. E = durable

Q5. C = underneath the rails

Q6. E = to fix any gap or void in the track alignment

Q7. D = alarms

Q8. B = to warn workers of an approaching train

Q9. Night

Q10. B = vibrations and D = noise

Q11. Manually, with the use of beaters

Q12. D = hardly ever

Q13. Ballast tamper

Q14. C = has been used for many years

TEST 2

You have 4 minutes only to read the following passage and take notes before answering the questions supplied by the tutor.

Freight trains are primarily used to transport cargo and goods, as opposed to transporting passengers. The railway network in Great Britain has been used to transport goods of various types and in various contingencies since the early 19th century. Whilst good traffic in the UK is considerably lower than other countries, it continues to be used, and continues to grow.

Rail freight has become extremely vital in regards to Britain's economic success. It is argued that using rail freight has contributed to over £800 million to the economy. Not only that, but it has also reduced congestion and carbon emissions, and therefore making this use of transportation more environmentally friendly.

Whether it is transporting raw materials for manufacturing purposes, fuels for electrical generations or consumer goods, businesses in the UK rely on freight trains to transport the cargo in an environmentally friendly and efficient way.

The UK has become more reliant on the use of rail freight which provides a faster, safer, greener and efficient way of transporting loads of cargo. It has been said that rail freight is expected to grow in demand by 30% in the next decade. This is equivalent to 240 additional freight trains per day.

In order to maintain and uphold this level of continual growth and demand for freight trains, train operating companies will work in partnership with the government to move cargo transports off of the road, and improve the quality of life by substantially reducing carbon emissions.

It is fact that, on average, a gallon of fuel will move a tonne of goods 246 miles on rail, but only 88 miles by road. Also, each freight train that is used, takes 60 HGV lorries off the road, ultimately helping carbon emissions.

During the First World War, it was renowned as the "Railway War". Thousands of tonnes of supplies and munitions were distributed all over Great Britain, whereby the supplies were dispatched from ports in the South East to be shipped over to France and the Front Line. A number of programmes were instigated in order for railways to meet the huge demands of the wartime. The Common User Agreement, conducted under the Coal Transport Act of 1917 are two examples of programmes that ultimately enabled better railway services. Over 100 train operating companies collaborated on these programmes and worked together in aid of national interest.

Question 1

What do freight trains carry?

    A – Passengers

    B – Cargo

    C – Passengers and cargo

    D – Cannot be determined

Answer [   ]

Question 2

How long has freight trains been in use in Great Britain?

    A – Early 17th century

    B – Late 17th century

    C – Early 18th century

    D – Late 18th century

    E – Early 19th century

Answer [   ]

Question 3

The use of rail freight for Britain has been extremely vital in regards to…

    A – Government success

    B – Train Operating Companies becoming more popular

    C – Economical success

    D – Transport safety

    E – Cannot be determined

Answer [   ]

Question 4

On average, how much has rail freight contributed to the economy?

A – £600 million

B – £800 million

C – £300 million

D – £500 million

E – £900 million

Answer [   ]

Question 5

Which two of the following answers can be concluded from rail freight being more environmentally friendly? Two answers required.

A – Reduces carbon emissions

B – Reduces the use of HGV's

C – Reduces cost

D – Reduces congestion

E – Reduces numerous transportation methods

Answer [   ]

Question 6

On average, a gallon of fuel for freight trains can move a tonne of goods how far?

A – 88 miles

B – 100 miles

C – 246 miles

D – 276 miles

E – 44 miles

Answer

Question 7

On average, a gallon of fuel for road usage can move a tonne of goods how far?

A – 246 miles

B – 44 miles

C – 102 miles

D – 88 miles

E – 70 miles

Answer

Question 8

If a freight train is used, how many HGV lorries are taken off the road?

    A – 40

    B – 60

    C – 30

    D – 70

    E – 80

Answer

Question 9

How much are freight trains expected to grow in demand within one decade?

    A – 20%

    B – 70%

    C – 50%

    D – 40%

    E – 30%

Answer

Question 10

If freight trains continue to grow at the rate that is expected, how many additional freight trains will be used per day?

A – 210

B – 240

C – 200

D – 180

E – 190

Answer

Question 11

How many train companies collaborated on the programmes that were instigated during the First World War?

A – Over 50

B – Over 60

C – Over 20

D – Over 80

E – Over 100

Answer

Question 12

What was the name of the Act that enabled better transport services during World War I?

    A – Coal Transport Act 1921

    B – Coal Transport Act 1917

    C – Coal Transport Act 1912

    D – Coal Transport Act 1931

    E – Coal Transport Act 1940

Answer

Question 13

What was the First World War also known as?

    A – Britain's War

    B – British Railway War

    C – Front Line War

    D – Railway War

    E – Cannot be determined

Answer

Question 14

Where were the supplies being shipped? Two answers required.

    A – Germany

    B – France

    C – Front Line

    D – England

    E – Cannot be determined

Answer

ANSWERS TO TEST 1, SECTION 2

Q1. B = cargo

Q2. E = early 19th century

Q3. C = economical success

Q4. B = £800 million

Q5. A = reduces carbon emissions, D = reduces congestion

Q6. C = 246 miles

Q7. D = 88 miles

Q8. B = 60

Q9. E = 30%

Q10. B = 240

Q11. E = over 100

Q12. B = Coal Transport Act 1917

Q13. D = Railway War

Q14. B = France, C = Front Line

TEST 3

You have 4 minutes only to read the following passage and take notes before answering the questions supplied by the tutor.

The railway system of Great Britain is one of the oldest in the world. The first steam locomotive was used in Britain's nation, and is is has become a paramount feature of contemporary society.

The arrival of railways has subsequently contributed to the dramatic growth in Industrialisation during the nineteenth century, and has ultimately had profound impacts on social and economical changes. The railway 'filled a void' in what other means of transport could not. Railways were able to provide an efficient, fast, cost effective and environmentally friendly service that catered for the needs of many people.

The history of the railways in Great Britain is remarkable. To see the incredible changes over hundreds of years is remarkable and can only be described as the 'transformation of transport'. In 1804, the first successful steam locomotive runs on wheels, and was used to transport iron across a track of nine miles. Built by Richard Trevithick's, the locomotive – 'the Penydarren', was the World's first steam engine to run on rails.

Since the early 19th century, railways have continued to develop and are now a strong infrastructure within hundreds of societies. During the First World War, the Government took over and run the railways until 1921, when private railway companies regained control. During 1921, an Act was passed in Parliament which submerged four railway companied: known simply as the 'British Rail'.

During 1940 in the Second World War, the companies effectively worked together to help Britain's war efforts, and in the late 1940's, these railways were nationalised and formed the 'British Railways', which was implemented under the Transport Act. In the 50's, society saw a modernised change in regards to railway services. Diesel and electrical trains were introduced and started to replace the steam locomotive trains.

In 1960, the railways were re-organised in hope to make money. Secondary routes and branch lines closed. As rationalisation took hold at this time, one-third of the pre-1948 networks had closed. A giant leap was undertaken in the 70's, and saw the introduction of the 'high-speed diesel-electric' service trains, and by 1990 both main coastal express routes, the East and West Coast Main Lines had been electrified between central Scotland and London.

In 1994, the Channel Tunnel opened and began the service from England to France. This exponential growth in regards to the railway services has considerably changed over the years, and is believed to continue to adapt.

In 2011, the number of journeys in Great Britain between 2010 and 2011 reaches a record breaking 1.16 billion, and by 2013, the railways are believed to be the second safest in Europe (after Luxembourg), and ultimately delivers a modernised service or both local and national railway routes.

Question 1

Where was the first steam locomotive train used?

A – China

B – Germany

C – France

D – Britain

E – Spain

Answer [   ]

Question 2

The railway was able to do what, that other transportation methods could not?

A – Create profits

B – Fill a void

C – Reduce carbon emissions

D – Help Industrialise society

E – Create transport for the middle classes

Answer [   ]

Question 3

In what year was the first running steam locomotive train made?

A – 1800

B – 1901

C – 1821

D – 1804

E – 1904

Answer [   ]

Question 4

What was the name of the 'mechanical genius' who built the first steam locomotive train?

Answer [ ]

Question 5

What was the first steam locomotive train called?

Answer [ ]

Question 6

In 1921, the railway service an Act in Parliament was implemented and saw the introduction of...

A – 'British Railways'

B – 'Great British Railways'

C – 'The four rails'

D – 'British Rail'

E – Cannot be determined

Answer [ ]

Question 7

What was the name of the Act in 1940 that nationalised the four railways?

A – Transportation Act

B – Local Transport Act

C – Transport Act

D – National Transport Act

E – Cannot be determined

Answer [ ]

Question 8

What fraction of the pre-1948 services closed in 1960?

A – One half

B – one quarter

C – One fifth

D – One third

E – Three thirds

Answer

Question 9

What type of trains were introduced in 1970?

A – High speed

B – Diesel

C – Electrical

D – Steam

E – All of the above

Answer

Question 10

What opened in 1994?

A – Medway Tunnel

B – Bradway Tunnel

C – The Channel Tunnel

D – Redhill Tunnel

E – Dartford Tunnel

Answer

Question 11

Between 2010 and 2011, the number of journeys reached a record breaking...

    A – 1.61 billion

    B – 1.16 billion

    C – 1.66 billion

    D – 1.16 million

    E – 6.16 billion

Answer

Question 12

What is the safest railway in Europe?

Answer

Question 13

What service does the Channel Tunnel offer? I.e. England to...?

Answer

Question 14

In what year did private train companies regain control of the railway services?

    A – 1984

    B – 1904

    C – 1911

    D – 1927

    E – 1921

Answer

ANSWERS TO TEST 1, SECTION 3

Q1. D = Britain

Q2. B = fill a void

Q3. D = 1804

Q4. Richard Trevithick

Q5. 'The Penydarren'

Q6. D = British Rail

Q7. C = Transport Act

Q8. D = one third

Q9. A = high speed

Q10. C = the Channel Tunnel

Q11. B = 1.16 billion

Q12. Luxembourg

Q13. France

Q14. E = 1921

CHECKING TEST –
TEST SECTION 1

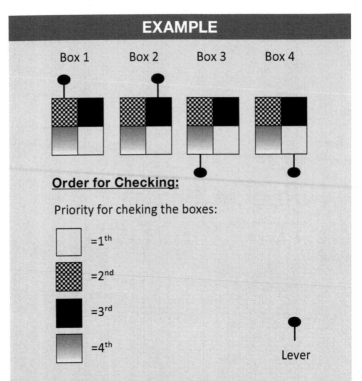

EXAMPLE

For these types of questions, it is important to take the time and carefully look at the key you are given.

- For the above example, you will notice that box 4 would need to be checked first. This is because the lever has been placed in a white box (which indicates that it needs to be first priority for checking).

- The next box that would need to be checked is box 1, then box 2, and then box 3.

Answer

4123

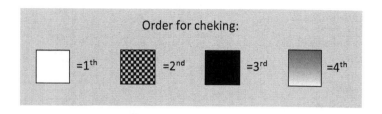

Order for cheking:

☐ =1th   ▦ =2nd   ■ =3rd   ▧ =4th

For the following ten questions, write down the order in which the boxes should be checked using the 'Order for Checking' sequence above:

Question 1

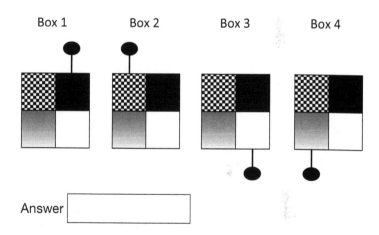

Box 1   Box 2   Box 3   Box 4

Answer

Question 2

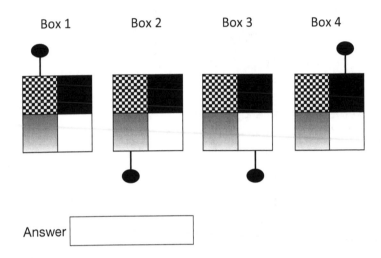

Answer

Question 3

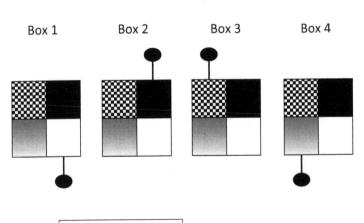

Answer

Question 4

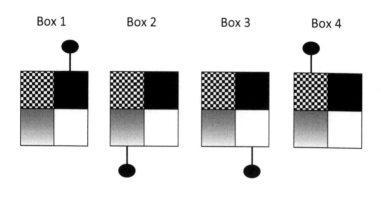

Answer [   ]

Question 5

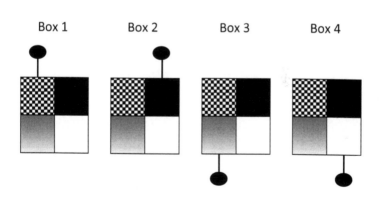

Answer [   ]

Question 6

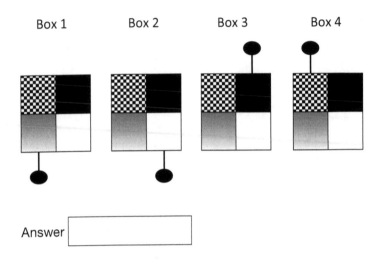

Answer

Question 7

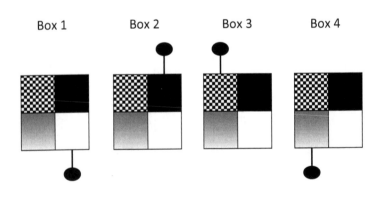

Answer

Question 8

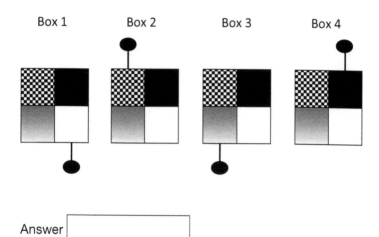

Answer

Question 9

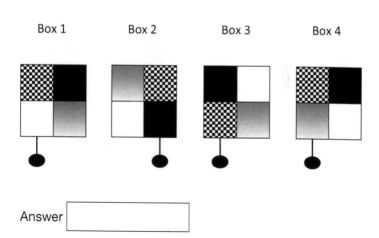

Answer

Question 10

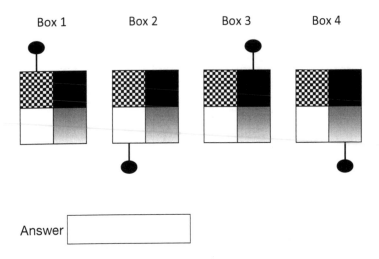

Answer [   ]

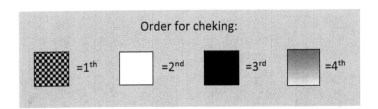

For the following ten questions, write down the order in which the boxes should be checked using the 'Order for Checking' sequence above:

Question 11

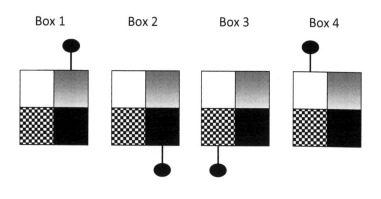

Answer [ ]

Question 12

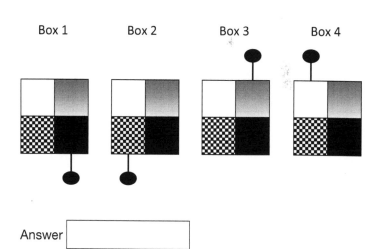

Answer [ ]

Question 13

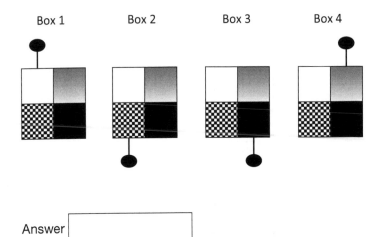

Answer

Question 14

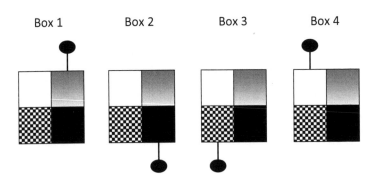

Answer

Question 15

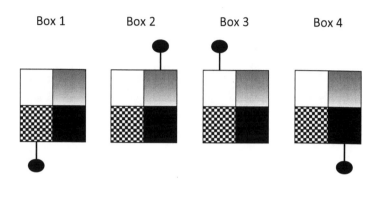

Answer

Question 16

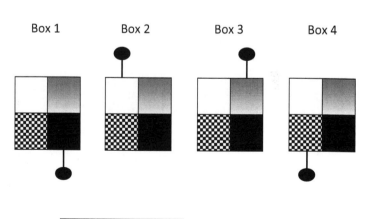

Answer

Question 17

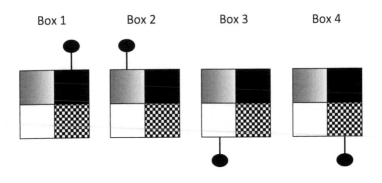

Answer [   ]

Question 18

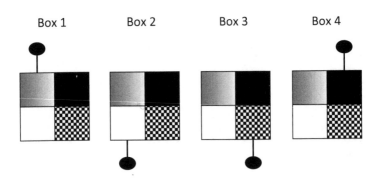

Answer [   ]

Question 19

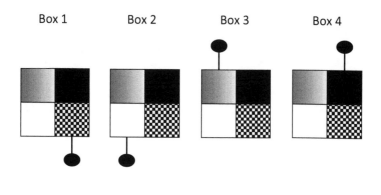

Answer [   ]

Question 20

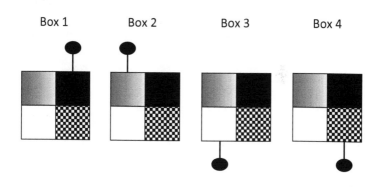

Answer [   ]

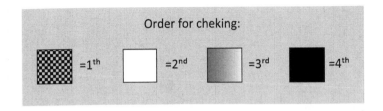

For the following five questions, write down the order in which the boxes should be checked using the 'Order for Checking' sequence above:

Question 21

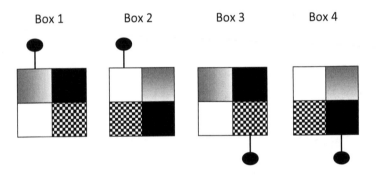

Answer [   ]

Question 22

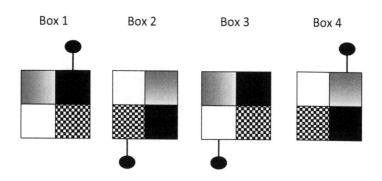

Answer [   ]

Question 23

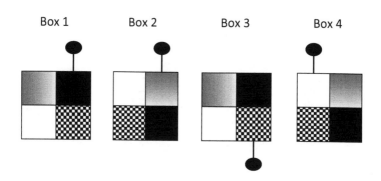

Answer [   ]

Question 24

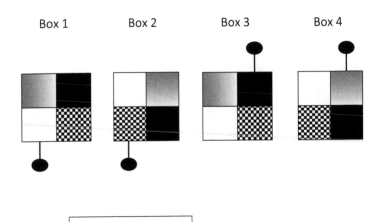

Answer [   ]

Question 25

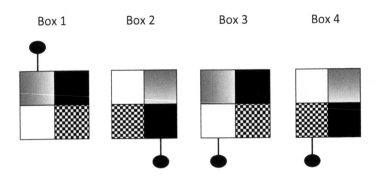

Answer [   ]

ANSWERS TO CHECKING TEST - TEST SECTION 1

Q1. 3214

Q2. 3142

Q3. 1324

Q4. 3412

Q5. 4123

Q6. 2431

Q7. 1324

Q8. 1243

Q9. 1324

Q10. 2134

Q11. 3421

Q12. 2413

Q13. 2134

Q14. 3421

Q15. 1342

Q16. 4213

Q17. 4312

Q18. 3241

Q19. 1243

Q20. 4312

Q21. 3214

Q22. 2341

Q23. 3421

Q24. 2143

Q25. 4312

FURTHER PRACTICE FOR CHECKING TESTS

In order to further assist you in your preparation for the Checking Test, I have created a sample Switch Analysis test. Although the test is different to the 'dials and cable' test that you encountered during the previous two tests, it will allow you to improve your skills in preparation for the real test.

In the following question you have to identify which of the three switches (W, Z or X) is not working. The box on the left hand side contains four circles, each labelled A, B, C and D. A key to the switches and the function they each perform is detailed below.

Question

Which switch in the sequence is not working?

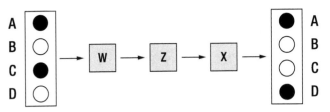

Switch	Function of the switch
W	Turns A and C on/off i.e. Black to white and vice versa
X	Turns B and D on/off i.e. Black to white and vice versa
Y	Turns C and D on/off i.e. Black to white and vice versa
Z	Turns A and D on/off i.e. Black to white and vice versa

You will notice that the box on the left contains black circles A and C, and white circles B and D at the start of the sequence. The first switch to operate is 'W', which has the effect of turning circles A and C from black to white, and vice versa. Once switch 'W' operates, the lights on the left will all be white in colour.

The next switch to operate is switch Z, which has the effect of turning circles A and D from black to white and vice versa. Because the circles contained within the box on the left hand side are all white after the operation of switch W, this now means that circles A and D are black, and circles B and C are white. You will notice that the box with the four circles located on the right hand side is now identical to this, which means that switch X must be inoperative. If it was working correctly, then the box of circles on the right hand side would look different. Therefore the correct answer to the question is switch X.

Now that you understand what is required during this test, take the time to work through the following sample Switch Analysis test. You have 5 minutes to complete the 10 questions.

SWITCH ANALYSIS TEST

Question 1

Which switch in the sequence is not working?

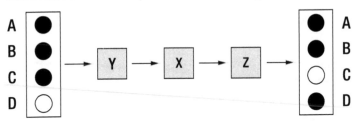

Switch	Function of the switch
W	Turns A and C on/off i.e. Black to white and vice versa
X	Turns B and D on/off i.e. Black to white and vice versa
Y	Turns C and D on/off i.e. Black to white and vice versa
Z	Turns A and D on/off i.e. Black to white and vice versa

Answer [   ]

Question 2

Which switch in the sequence is not working?

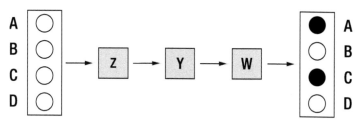

Switch	Function of the switch
W	Turns A and C on/off i.e. Black to white and vice versa
X	Turns B and D on/off i.e. Black to white and vice versa
Y	Turns C and D on/off i.e. Black to white and vice versa
Z	Turns A and D on/off i.e. Black to white and vice versa

Answer [   ]

Question 3

Which switch in the sequence is not working?

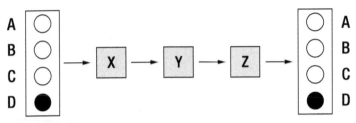

Switch	Function of the switch
W	Turns A and C on/off i.e. Black to white and vice versa
X	Turns B and D on/off i.e. Black to white and vice versa
Y	Turns C and D on/off i.e. Black to white and vice versa
Z	Turns A and D on/off i.e. Black to white and vice versa

Answer [　　　　　　　]

Question 4

Which switch in the sequence is not working?

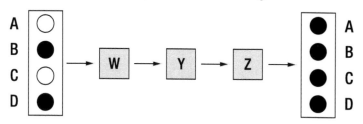

Switch	Function of the switch
W	Turns A and C on/off i.e. Black to white and vice versa
X	Turns B and D on/off i.e. Black to white and vice versa
Y	Turns C and D on/off i.e. Black to white and vice versa
Z	Turns A and D on/off i.e. Black to white and vice versa

Answer [   ]

Question 5

Which switch in the sequence is not working?

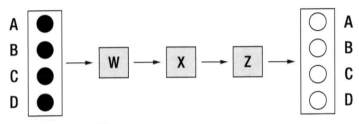

Switch	Function of the switch
W	Turns A and C on/off i.e. Black to white and vice versa
X	Turns B and D on/off i.e. Black to white and vice versa
Y	Turns C and D on/off i.e. Black to white and vice versa
Z	Turns A and D on/off i.e. Black to white and vice versa

Answer [   ]

Question 6

Which switch in the sequence is not working?

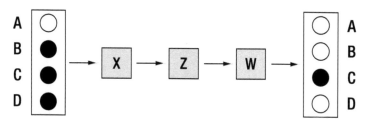

Switch	Function of the switch
W	Turns A and C on/off i.e. Black to white and vice versa
X	Turns B and D on/off i.e. Black to white and vice versa
Y	Turns C and D on/off i.e. Black to white and vice versa
Z	Turns A and D on/off i.e. Black to white and vice versa

Answer [   ]

Question 7

Which switch in the sequence is not working?

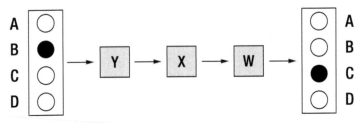

Switch	Function of the switch
W	Turns A and C on/off i.e. Black to white and vice versa
X	Turns B and D on/off i.e. Black to white and vice versa
Y	Turns C and D on/off i.e. Black to white and vice versa
Z	Turns A and D on/off i.e. Black to white and vice versa

Answer [   ]

Question 8

Which switch in the sequence is not working?

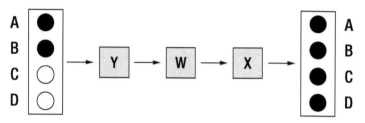

Switch	Function of the switch
W	Turns A and C on/off i.e. Black to white and vice versa
X	Turns B and D on/off i.e. Black to white and vice versa
Y	Turns C and D on/off i.e. Black to white and vice versa
Z	Turns A and D on/off i.e. Black to white and vice versa

Answer [   ]

Question 9

Which switch in the sequence is not working?

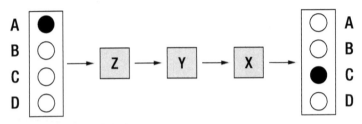

Switch	Function of the switch
W	Turns A and C on/off i.e. Black to white and vice versa
X	Turns B and D on/off i.e. Black to white and vice versa
Y	Turns C and D on/off i.e. Black to white and vice versa
Z	Turns A and D on/off i.e. Black to white and vice versa

Answer [   ]

Question 10

Which switch in the sequence is not working?

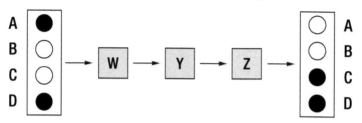

Switch	Function of the switch
W	Turns A and C on/off i.e. Black to white and vice versa
X	Turns B and D on/off i.e. Black to white and vice versa
Y	Turns C and D on/off i.e. Black to white and vice versa
Z	Turns A and D on/off i.e. Black to white and vice versa

Answer [   ]

ANSWERS TO FAULT ANALYSIS TEST

1. Switch X

2. Switch W

3. Switch X

4. Switch Y

5. Switch Z

6. Switch Z

7. Switch W

8. Switch W

9. Switch X

10. Switch Y

THE DOT CONCENTRATION TEST

The Dot Concentration Test is probably the hardest part of the psychometric testing process. It is the one test that most people fail and this is mainly due to a lack of preparation. Many candidates turn up to take the test without any prior knowledge of how it works and what is expected of them.

The test is designed to assess your ability to concentrate whilst performing tasks at high speed. The test will be carried out either with a pen and paper, or a computer and a computer screen. Whichever test you undertake, you will be presented with five pages or screens that each contains 25 columns. Each of the columns contains boxes with patterns of dots which are either in groups of 3, 4, 5 or 6. Your task is to work quickly and accurately through each column, from left to right, identifying boxes of 4 dots only.

You are allowed two minutes only per sheet and, once the two minutes are up, you are told to move onto the next page regardless of whether you have completed it or not. The test requires ten minutes of solid concentration.

Take a look at the following row of dots:

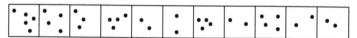

You will notice that the 2nd, 4th, 7th and 9th boxes each contain 4 dots. If you were taking the paper and pencil based version of the test, you would mark the boxes that contain 4 dots as follows:

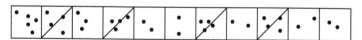

You will notice that I have placed a single diagonal line through each of the boxes that contains 4 dots.

If you are required to undertake the computer based version of the test then you will be required to use the keys on the keyboard as follows:

You will use this key to move from left to right across the screen.

You will use this key to mark each box that contains 4 dots.

You will use this key to move back in order to correct any mistakes.

On the following pages I have provided you with ten sample concentration tests. During the first set of five concentration tests you are required to locate specific letters and/or numbers that are contained within rows and columns. Full instructions are provided at the start of each test.

During the second set of five Dot Concentration tests you will be required to search for groups of 4 dots in rows and columns of boxes. Once again, full instructions are provided.

SAMPLE CONCENTRATION TEST 1

Cross out the letter 'R' (upper case) in each row. Write down the total number that you cross out in each row in the box provided at the end of each row. You have 60 seconds to complete the test.

1.	Q	r	R	g	y	U	h	J	R	j	R	k	L	B	n	
2.	R	R	R	v	B	n	M	U	u	d	f	O	p	T	R	
3.	C	x	X	F	R	G	t	p	A	R	f	V	R	y	U	
4.	Q	R	R	t	G	N	H	J	r	r	F	P	F	R	r	
5.	Q	a	Z	x	R	t	l	o	M	B	R	D	x	A	S	
6.	R	s	a	A	e	E	R	C	Y	U	r	j	P	o	R	
7.	T	R	r	P	F	r	S	N	b	V	c	F	F	R	R	
8.	G	v	R	r	R	y	R	P	R	r	D	e	E	R	F	
9.	T	R	K	P	o	u	b	g	t	m	R	r	X	r	R	
10.	C	B	n	h	j	Y	l	p	R	R	R	r	R	C	d	
11.	R	R	r	Y	u	B	v	M	n	h	K	j	R	E	R	
12.	A	W	r	E	R	f	p	U	l	H	R	y	U	B	R	
13.	R	r	Q	q	B	G	R	t	Q	w	E	F	T	y	R	
14.	T	R	A	l	N	D	P	l	V	E	R	D	T	y	S	
15.	d	x	z	Z	R	n	K	i	i	R	r	R	O	p	o	
16.	Q	R	r	E	D	D	e	w	K	i	l	O	P	R	R	
17.	H	O	w	B	e	E	R	r	R	R	V	R	H	j	R	
18.	K	j	u	U	Y	i	Y	r	R	R	D	X	z	q	Q	
19.	P	y	g	h	j	l	r	t	r	e	R	e	R	q	Z	
20.	B	h	B	h	r	r	R	r	N	B	H	y	Y	R	F	

SAMPLE CONCENTRATION TEST 2

Cross out the letter 'o' (lower case). Write down the total number that you cross out in each row in the box provided at the end of each row. You have 60 seconds to complete the test.

1.	o	O	t	Q	w	q	O	o	A	B	u	U	o	o	O	
2.	O	o	g	Y	t	B	c	C	c	O	o	o	o	D	w	
3.	B	o	O	g	a	s	S	q	Q	t	Q	q	O	o	G	
4.	I	L	N	h	U	u	O	o	H	y	t	R	o	O	o	
5.	G	V	v	R	t	Y	o	o	P	i	O	O	o	O	R	
6.	G	t	y	U	J	P	p	O	o	D	d	O	o	S	Q	
7.	O	o	O	o	o	o	Y	t	Y	q	Q	q	o	c	c	
8.	I	u	V	c	c	F	r	d	w	H	y	h	u	o	o	
9.	Y	o	o	U	o	O	O	y	D	e	q	A	q	O	o	
10.	R	r	t	o	u	y	G	b	t	r	e	o	o	o	P	
11.	o	O	c	o	d	d	D	O	c	c	O	o	o	d	R	
12.	B	v	c	f	R	o	y	f	D	r	d	r	a	A	a	
13.	F	t	t	t	d	r	e	o	o	p	u	o	Q	t	r	
14.	F	g	r	t	y	N	H	N	h	o	p	O	o	I	y	
15.	T	r	e	d	w	o	u	i	y	F	c	r	D	e	W	
16.	o	o	O	o	p	O	u	i	S	t	d	r	s	S	O	
17.	I	o	O	A	a	a	c	C	c	g	o	o	o	R	t	
18.	G	g	g	g	o	t	f	d	r	t	u	u	o	o	j	
19.	Q	c	v	b	g	t	y	u	O	o	O	o	G	y	c	
20.	K	I	o	i	u	y	t	r	e	o	u	y	o	j	h	

SAMPLE CONCENTRATION TEST 3

Cross out the letters 'w' (lower case) and 'V' (upper case). Search for both of these letters at the same time. Write down the total combined number that you cross out in each row in the box provided at the end of each row. You have 60 seconds to complete the test.

1.	v	W	w	V	e	w	h	j	U	i	X	x	W	w	v	
2.	V	u	U	w	G	t	y	u	W	w	V	v	W	o	o	
3.	W	W	V	V	v	v	w	w	y	u	i	p	v	W	W	
4.	V	g	h	j	K	O	p	t	Y	V	v	W	W	w	V	
5.	Y	U	u	u	v	v	W	M	m	w	e	V	v	N	n	
6.	q	q	Q	G	g	H	Y	u	i	R	T	y	V	w	v	
7.	V	y	u	Y	u	o	p	N	h	j	W	w	V	V	v	
8.	t	y	m	k	m	N	b	C	x	W	w	V	v	b	v	
9.	O	o	V	v	f	g	h	j	k	n	h	N	h	V	X	
10.	T	V	v	X	c	d	W	w	W	v	V	v	f	r	p	
11.	V	V	v	w	W	w	v	V	v	W	w	g	y	Y	v	
12.	R	t	y	u	i	B	g	v	f	r	D	r	Q	w	W	
13.	R	t	y	V	c	V	c	v	f	r	W	w	W	w	V	
14.	G	y	u	i	O	p	R	t	y	E	w	V	V	v	W	
15.	Y	Y	y	Y	X	v	W	W	w	w	r	t	y	u	v	
16.	W	w	w	v	t	u	i	n	h	v	V	w	W	w	f	
17.	r	t	y	y	u	i	V	b	n	h	g	w	w	W	w	
18.	i	o	q	w	S	S	X	W	V	Z	z	V	v	W	y	
19.	P	o	Y	u	i	V	v	X	w	W	w	R	t	R	y	
20.	y	u	V	x	s	t	Y	u	y	W	w	C	d	V	w	

SAMPLE CONCENTRATION TEST 4

Cross out the number 8 and the letter 'b' (lower case). Search for both letter and number at the same time. Write down the total combined number that you cross out in each row in the box provided at the end of each row. You have 60 seconds to complete the test.

1.	8	B	8	V	v	W	q	P	p	r	g	B	b	8	u	
2.	B	b	R	r	r	y	U	i	8	8	B	B	b	g	G	
3.	j	u	p	P	b	v	f	r	B	b	w	3	6	7	R	
4.	8	3	2	h	y	U	x	W	w	v	x	v	b	B	8	
5.	f	G	g	B	p	h	b	b	b	B	B	8	8	5	3	
6.	y	u	U	7	6	5	8	e	r	d	r	w	8	B	b	
7.	o	O	o	P	7	8	5	b	3	8	3	R	r	S	l	
8.	B	b	3	8	B	B	b	h	h	V	c	b	B	7	1	
9.	1	3	c	V	f	I	u	y	t	r	B	b	8	8	8	
10.	y	B	b	8	4	3	3	3	X	x	x	f	F	r	t	
11.	Q	q	H	b	B	b	8	B	6	3	3	2	u	B	b	
12.	G	G	g	B	b	8	3	8	3	D	d	D	I	P	p	
13.	G	b	b	8	8	6	5	4	0	L	o	P	p	P	B	
14.	3	B	b	8	3	B	B	b	3	E	e	3	8	4	P	
15.	t	Y	y	D	e	e	D	f	g	W	8	8	P	P	B	
16.	C	C	b	n	B	8	B	8	B	b	8	3	9	3	9	
17.	6	6	b	B	8	8	d	k	I	p	o	U	S	y	Y	
18.	P	p	8	F	d	D	c	C	8	B	b	8	f	F	f	
19.	8	8	C	f	z	s	W	w	R	r	T	8	3	B	b	
20.	H	y	y	b	B	8	8	8	H	H	h	D	r	e	W	

SAMPLE CONCENTRATION TEST 5

Cross out the letter 'e' (lower case) and the number '3'.
Search for both letter and number at the same time. Write
down the number crossed out in the box provided at the
end of each row. You have 60 seconds to complete the test.

1.	E	6	e	8	8	e	3	p	b	d	e	E	3	8	T	
2.	e	8	3	6	7	y	u	I	V	f	E	e	b	B	E	
3.	W	w	q	D	d	c	x	z	O	p	e	R	6	8	3	
4.	y	u	I	o	p	P	t	T	Y	e	E	3	8	6	F	
5.	g	B	4	3	2	7	8	3	e	E	3	4	E	e	3	
6.	e	3	3	e	E	d	W	q	h	j	K	8	7	N	9	
7.	3	e	E	8	B	8	3	e	E	k	K	3	e	8	7	
8.	f	C	x	b	g	t	T	r	6	8	3	4	X	d	e	
9.	3	3	3	b	8	b	e	3	E	3	8	3	4	0	1	
10.	e	E	j	H	g	b	3	E	e	3	w	b	V	v	E	
11.	8	3	B	v	C	f	v	e	8	4	3	3	3	e	v	
12.	6	7	8	v	c	D	f	3	7	8	6	E	e	e	V	
13.	e	3	e	3	E	8	E	3	e	E	3	2	8	G	g	
14.	7	y	h	n	g	f	d	e	E	4	E	e	3	D	d	
15.	k	I	L	j	h	y	V	v	8	4	2	b	V	v	E	
16.	g	Y	y	i	9	8	7	0	3	O	o	v	V	v	e	
17.	8	2	B	b	v	e	W	e	r	5	5	R	r	e	V	
18.	3	e	E	e	3	4	b	V	v	e	W	w	q	A	a	
19.	5	e	3	V	f	r	6	5	4	e	e	E	e	3	E	
20.	e	E	e	R	3	4	2	1	3	E	e	h	G	f	d	

ANSWERS TO CONCENTRATION TESTS

Test 1

1.	3	6.	3	11.	4	16.	3
2.	4	7.	3	12.	3	17.	5
3.	3	8.	5	13.	3	18.	2
4.	3	9.	3	14.	2	19.	2
5.	2	10.	4	15.	3	20.	2

Test 2

1.	4	6.	2	11.	4	16.	3
2.	4	7.	5	12.	1	17.	4
3.	2	8.	2	13.	3	18.	3
4.	3	9.	4	14.	2	19.	2
5.	3	10.	4	15.	1	20.	3

Test 3

1.	4	6.	2	11.	6	16.	5
2.	4	7.	4	12.	1	17.	4
3.	4	8.	2	13.	5	18.	3
4.	4	9.	2	14.	3	19.	3
5.	2	10.	3	15.	2	20.	4

Test 4

1.	4	6.	3	11.	4	16.	5
2.	4	7.	3	12.	3	17.	3
3.	2	8.	4	13.	4	18.	4
4.	3	9.	4	14.	4	19.	4
5.	5	10.	2	15.	2	20.	4

Test 5

1.	5	6.	4	11.	6	16.	2
2.	3	7.	6	12.	3	17.	3
3.	2	8.	2	13.	7	18.	5
4.	2	9.	7	14.	3	19.	6
5.	6	10.	4	15.	0	20.	5

Check through your answers carefully and go back to check over the ones you got wrong.

Now move onto to the next set of five Dot Concentration' tests.

SAMPLE DOT CONCENTRATION TEST 1

Place a diagonal line across each box that contains 4 dots only. You have 30 seconds to complete the test

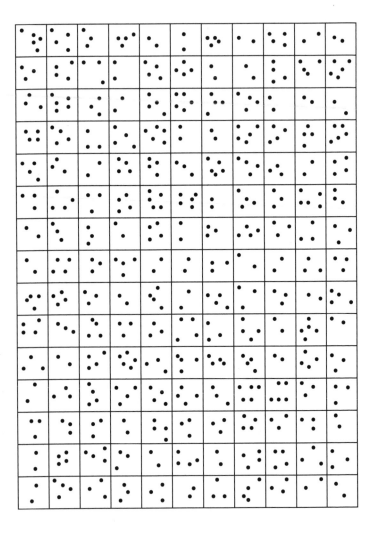

SAMPLE DOT CONCENTRATION TEST 2

Place a diagonal line across each box that contains 4 dots only. You have 30 seconds to complete the test.

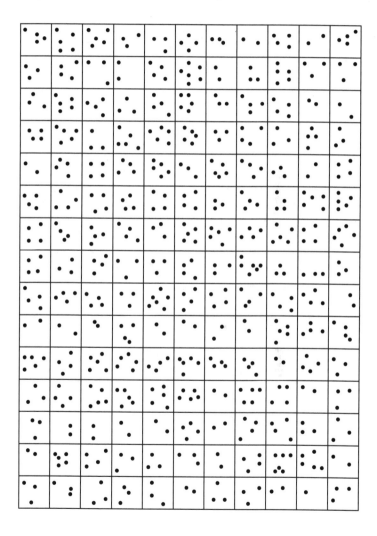

SAMPLE DOT CONCENTRATION TEST 3

Place a diagonal line across each box that contains 4 dots only. You have 30 seconds to complete the test.

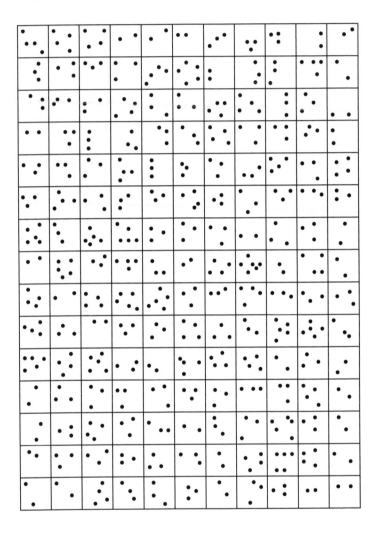

SAMPLE DOT CONCENTRATION TEST 4

Place a diagonal line across each box that contains 4 dots only. You have 30 seconds to complete the test.

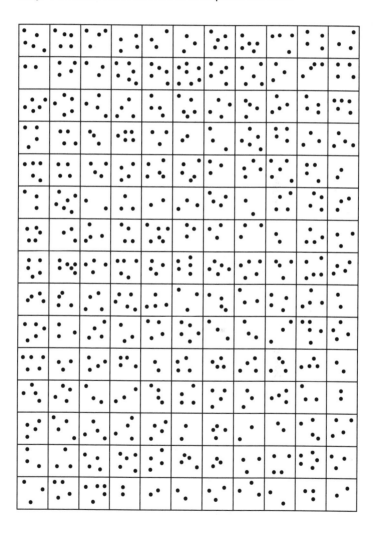

SAMPLE DOT CONCENTRATION TEST 5

Place a diagonal line across each box that contains 4 dots only. You have 30 seconds to complete the test.

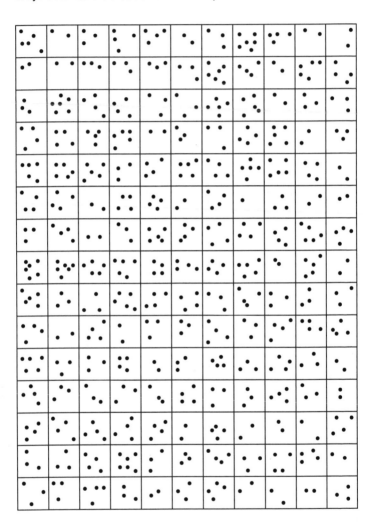

ANSWERS TO DOT CONCENTRATION TESTS 1 TO 5

Dot Concentration Test 1

56 boxes containing groups of 4 dots

Dot Concentration Test 2

58 boxes containing groups of 4 dots

Dot Concentration Test 3

31 boxes containing groups of 4 dots

Dot Concentration Test 4

66 boxes containing groups of 4 dots

Dot Concentration Test 5

56 boxes containing groups of 4 dots

TRAIN DRIVER ERROR CHECKING TEST (TD-ECT)

During your Train Driver assessment, you will also be expected to take a test that is designed to assess the key skills and qualities required by anyone who wishes to become a Train Driver. As an aspiring Train Driver, you will need to demonstrate high levels of skills in the following areas:

- Concentration
- Attention to detail
- Awareness
- Perseverance

The Train Driver Error Checking Test (TD-ECT) is a test primarily designed to assess these particular areas in order to improve your overall performance. Created by How2become, this Train Driver practice test allows you to practice and prepare for your assessment. *Please note, that whilst we have provided practice questions, the Train Driver Error Checking Test (TD-ECT) is not an official Train Driving test.* It is a test created by our team for you to gain a clearer understanding of the nature in which you'll be tested, and the typical skills that are often evaluated.

About the Train Driver Error Checking Test (TD-ECT)

The Train Driver Error Checking Test is an assessment that allows aspiring Train Drivers to practice their skills in order to prepare them for their assessment. The test measures particular skills, mostly focussing on concentration ability and attention to detail. These skills will be put to the test by measuring a person's ability to recognise errors in diagram formations.

Becoming a Train Driver requires a great deal of perseverance, and much of that perseverance comes from practicing. The more a person practices prior to their assessment, the more comfortable and confident they will feel in regards to their test. Thus, it is imperative that, whilst we cannot provide an exact account of what to expect in your actual test, we can provide questions that will focus on the necessary skills and qualities Train Drivers must possess in order to be successful during the selection process.

SAMPLE QUESTION

In order to answer the following questions, you must become familiar with the structure and format. You will need to apply rules and instructions to the questions in order to assess the error that is present.

During these practice questions, you will be given a set of diagrams for which you need to find the errors, using the Error Code Chart provided. The Error Code Chart are the codes that you will need to use to answer all of the questions.

The Error Code Chart will remain the same throughout the test, and is shown below:

Error Code Chart			
Front Tyre	Rear Tyre	Brake Pads	Lights
FT	RT	BP	L

You will then be given 5 questions based on an Error Reference Chart. This will need to be used and remembered to determine which errors the bicycles have. The bicycles may have one or more errors. You will be able to work out the errors based on the reference codes and whether they are the same. If the bicycle does not have the same reference code, then there is an error.

The Error Reference Chart is formulated below:

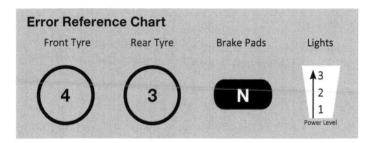

Using the Error Reference Chart, you must place the correct error code for each question. For Each Reference Chart, it will contain 5 questions. You will need to work out where the errors lie in the diagram.

Using the above Error Reference Chart, and using the Error Codes, find the error in the following diagram.

This is the order that you need to use to check each part of the bicycle. *The Order for Checking changes, so be sure to pay attention to this!*

Using the Error Codes (FT, RT, BP, L), you will need to put your answers in the report, in order of Checking, filling in the box where an error has occurred.

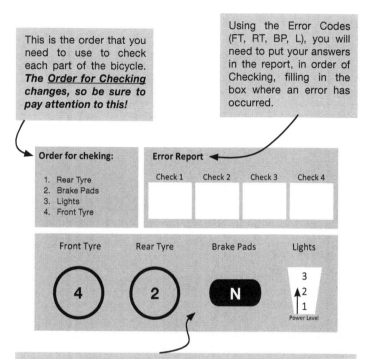

Order for cheking:

1. Rear Tyre
2. Brake Pads
3. Lights
4. Front Tyre

Error Report

Check 1	Check 2	Check 3	Check 4

Front Tyre	Rear Tyre	Brake Pads	Lights
4	2	N	3 / 2 / 1 Power Level

This set of diagrams need to be analysed carefully. You will have been given a Reference Chart to study before the question. Your task is to use that Reference Chart and cross-reference any errors in this set of diagrams. If a reference is different in the question, compared to that found on the Reference Chart, which means there is an error, and you would need to write it in your report.

ANSWER FOR SAMPLE QUESTION:

Error Report			
Check 1	Check 2	Check 3	Check 4
RT	**-**	**L**	**-**

- For Check 1, using the order for checking, you need to check the Rear Tyre. Using the Reference Chart, the Rear Tyre is referenced '3', whereas in the question it is referenced '2'. This shows an error, because the references do not match. Therefore, you would need to write RT in the Check 1 box.

- For Check 2, using the order for checking, you would need to check the Brake Pads. Using the Reference Chart, the Brake Pads are referenced 'N'; in the question, the Brake Pads are also referenced 'N', therefore shows no error. In order to mark no error in the box', simply put a line through the box.

- For Check 3, using the order for checking, you would need to check the Lights. Using the Reference Chart, the Lights are referenced with the power '1-3'; in the question the Lights are only powered to '2'. This shows an error, because the references do not match. Therefore, you would to write L in the Check 3 box.

- For Check 4, using the order for checking, you would need to check the Front Tyre. Using the Reference Chart, the Front Tyre is referenced '4;' in the question, the Front Tyre is also referenced '4'. This shows no error, and you should draw a line through the box, indicating that there is no error.

Using the above system, work through the 60 questions as quickly and as effectively as you can. Remember, the point of these types of questions is to measure speed, as well as accuracy.

Make sure that you read all the information on the Reference Chart, before attempting to answer the six questions that relate. For each question, it is vitally important that you check what order you need to assess first. You will lose easy marks for lack of attention to detail.

Error Code Chart

Front Tyre	Rear Tyre	Brake Pads	Lights
FT	**RT**	**BP**	**L**

The above Chart is a reminder of the Error Codes that you will need to insert into the Error Report for each error you find.

Error Reference Chart

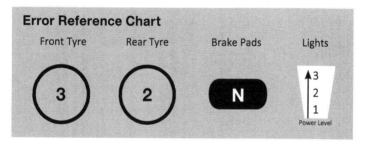

Front Tyre	Rear Tyre	Brake Pads	Lights
3	2	N	Power Level: 3 2 1

Using the Error Reference Chart below, answer questions 1 to 6, based on the information found in this chart.

For the **next 6 questions**, use the above Error Reference Chart to determine which errors the bicycle have. If the bicycle does not have the same reference, then there is an error.

Only enter a code if there is an error present! If an error is not present, draw a line through the box.

Question 1

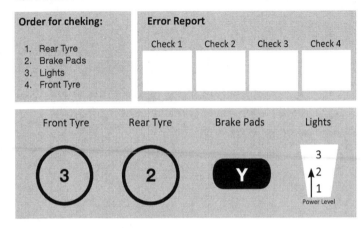

Question 2

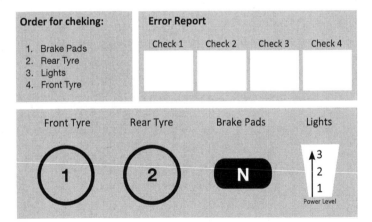

Question 3

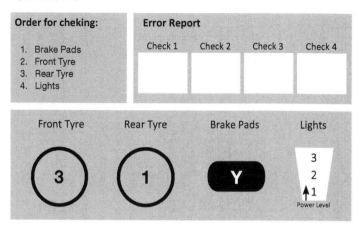

Order for cheking:

1. Brake Pads
2. Front Tyre
3. Rear Tyre
4. Lights

Error Report

Check 1	Check 2	Check 3	Check 4

Front Tyre	Rear Tyre	Brake Pads	Lights
3	1	Y	3 2 ↑1 Power Level

Question 4

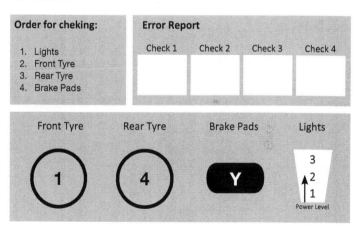

Order for cheking:

1. Lights
2. Front Tyre
3. Rear Tyre
4. Brake Pads

Error Report

Check 1	Check 2	Check 3	Check 4

Front Tyre	Rear Tyre	Brake Pads	Lights
1	4	Y	3 ↑2 1 Power Level

Question 5

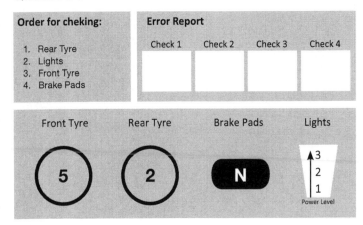

Order for cheking:

1. Rear Tyre
2. Lights
3. Front Tyre
4. Brake Pads

Error Report

Check 1	Check 2	Check 3	Check 4

Front Tyre	Rear Tyre	Brake Pads	Lights
5	2	N	Power Level: 3 2 1

Question 6

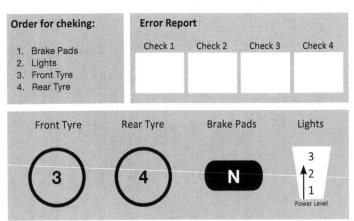

Order for cheking:

1. Brake Pads
2. Lights
3. Front Tyre
4. Rear Tyre

Error Report

Check 1	Check 2	Check 3	Check 4

Front Tyre	Rear Tyre	Brake Pads	Lights
3	4	N	Power Level: 3 2 1

Error Code Chart

Front Tyre	Rear Tyre	Brake Pads	Lights
FT	RT	BP	L

The above Chart is a reminder of the Error Codes that you will need to insert into the Error Report for each error you find.

Error Reference Chart

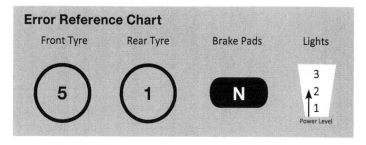

Front Tyre — Rear Tyre — Brake Pads — Lights

Using the Error Reference Chart below, answer questions 7 to 12, based on the information found in this chart.

For the **next 6 questions**, use the above Error Reference Chart to determine which errors the bicycle have. If the bicycle does not have the same reference, then there is an error.

Only enter a code if there is an error present! If an error is not present, draw a line through the box.

Question 7

Order for cheking:	Error Report			
1. Rear Tyre 2. Lights 3. Front Tyre 4. Brake Pads	Check 1	Check 2	Check 3	Check 4

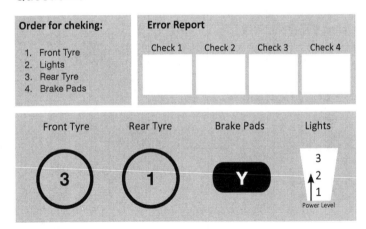

Question 8

Order for cheking:	Error Report			
1. Front Tyre 2. Lights 3. Rear Tyre 4. Brake Pads	Check 1	Check 2	Check 3	Check 4

Question 9

Order for cheking:	Error Report			
1. Front Tyre 2. Lights 3. Rear Tyre 4. Brake Pads	Check 1	Check 2	Check 3	Check 4

Front Tyre	Rear Tyre	Brake Pads	Lights
5	5	N	3 2 1 Power Level

Question 10

Order for cheking:	Error Report			
1. Brake Pads 2. Rear Tyre 3. Lights 4. Front Tyre	Check 1	Check 2	Check 3	Check 4

Front Tyre	Rear Tyre	Brake Pads	Lights
4	1	N	3 2 1 Power Level

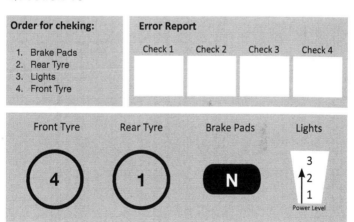

Question 11

Order for cheking:

1. Brake Pads
2. Front Tyre
3. Lights
4. Rear Tyre

Error Report

Check 1	Check 2	Check 3	Check 4

Front Tyre	Rear Tyre	Brake Pads	Lights
5	1	Y	3 2 1 Power Level

Question 12

Order for cheking:

1. Lights
2. Rear Tyre
3. Brake Pads
4. Front Tyre

Error Report

Check 1	Check 2	Check 3	Check 4

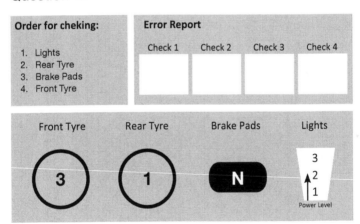

Front Tyre	Rear Tyre	Brake Pads	Lights
3	1	N	3 2 1 Power Level

ANSWERS TO TRAIN DRIVER ERROR CHECKING TEST – (SECTION 1)

Question 1.

Error Report			
Check 1	Check 2	Check 3	Check 4
-	**BP**	**L**	-

Question 2.

Error Report			
Check 1	Check 2	Check 3	Check 4
-	-	-	**FT**

Question 3.

Error Report			
Check 1	Check 2	Check 3	Check 4
BP	-	**RT**	**L**

Question 4.

Error Report			
Check 1	Check 2	Check 3	Check 4
L	**FT**	**RT**	**BP**

Question 5.

Error Report			
Check 1	Check 2	Check 3	Check 4
-	-	**FT**	-

Question 6.

Error Report			
Check 1	Check 2	Check 3	Check 4
-	**L**	-	**RT**

Question 7.

Error Report			
Check 1	Check 2	Check 3	Check 4
RT	**L**	-	**BP**

Question 8.

Error Report			
Check 1	Check 2	Check 3	Check 4
FT	-	-	**BP**

Question 9.

Error Report			
Check 1	Check 2	Check 3	Check 4
-	-	**RT**	-

Question 10.

Error Report			
Check 1	Check 2	Check 3	Check 4
-	-	**L**	**FT**

Question 11.

Error Report			
Check 1	Check 2	Check 3	Check 4
BP	-	**L**	-

Question 12.

Error Report			
Check 1	Check 2	Check 3	Check 4
-	-	-	**FT**

THE FAST REACTION
AND CO-ORDINATION TEST

The final part of the psychometric testing is the Fast Reaction and Co-ordination Test. You will be provided with a computer, a monitor, a modified keyboard, a set of foot pedals, and some headphones. The test is designed to assess your ability to react to specific instructions that are transmitted either through your headphones or via the computer screen. The keyboard has been modified and will have a number of colour coded buttons and two separate buttons that indicate the words 'HI' and 'LO'. When the test begins you will see a number of different flashing colours appear on the screen. Your task is to press the same colour button on the keyboard whenever you see the appropriate colour on the screen. At the same time you will also hear either a high-pitch tone or low-pitch tone through your headphones. As soon as you hear the tone you must press either the 'HI' button or the 'LO' button depending on the tone you hear. In addition to this, you will also see coloured boxes appear in the bottom left and right hand corners of the screen. When you see these boxes you must press down the relevant foot pedal that the button corresponds with.

Before the actual test commences you will have two practice runs. Make sure you take deep breaths whilst performing the practice tests and remain as calm as possible. You will find that if you panic you will start to make too many mistakes. During the actual test you will have to undertake two 6-minute tests. As the test progresses, so does the speed at which you will have to react. Don't worry if you start to make mistakes. Just try to recover and continue where you left off. This type of test is very difficult to prepare for. However, there is a toy called 'Bop It' that is a useful practice aid that utilises your hands and listening skills. The 'Bop It' can be purchased by visiting www.firebox.com and then typing the words 'bop it' into the search bar. The toy can also be purchased at all good toy stores or through Amazon.co.uk.

how2become

Visit www.how2become.com to find more titles and courses that will help you to pass the Train Driver selection process, including:

- How to pass the Train Driver interview DVD.

- 1 Day Train Driver course.

- Psychometric testing books and CDs.

www.how2become.com